The Unfinished Agenda

The Unfinished Agenda

Essays on the political economy
of government policy
in honour of Arthur Seldon

Ralph Harris · **Gordon Tullock** · **James Buchanan**

W. H. Hutt · **Basil Yamey** · **Ronald Coase**

Israel Kirzner · **Patrick Minford** · **Alan Walters**

Milton Friedman · **F. A. Hayek**

Edited by Martin J. Anderson

Published by
THE INSTITUTE OF ECONOMIC AFFAIRS
1986

First published in June 1986

by

THE INSTITUTE OF ECONOMIC AFFAIRS

2 Lord North Street, Westminster,

London SW1P 3LB

ISBN 0-255 36191-2

Printed in Great Britain by

GORON PRO-PRINT CO LTD

6 Marlborough Road, Churchill Industrial Estate, Lancing, W. Sussex

Text set in 'Monotype' Baskerville

Contents

Preface

MARTIN J. ANDERSON

IT has often been claimed by outside observers, sympathetic and hostile alike, that perhaps the most significant factor in the 'resurrection' of market economics in the discussion of government policy in the United Kingdom and, to an extent, abroad has been the activities of the Institute of Economic Affairs. If that is true, much of the credit for this astonishing transformation in the intellectual and political climate, if not yet in policy, can be laid at the door of one man. In the 30 years from the inception of the IEA in the mid-1950s to the present day the shape and content of its publication programme have been decided by Arthur Seldon. In liberal consultation with his colleague Ralph Harris, he has turned the attention of probably tens of thousands of professional and lay econ-omists away from a fashionable and unhealthy obsession with macro-economics to examine the more realistic micro-world of changing prices, unpredictable demand and imperfect markets, both private and state.

These are large claims, but it is certainly true that when the IEA was founded the voices of the sympathisers were far outnumbered by those who offered scepticism or even down-right disbelief. Arthur Seldon's unflagging efforts over the three decades that have brought him to his seventieth birthday have resulted in a list of titles well over 300 strong, all written to editorial standards (not least of comprehensibility) that were rare in economics until that now-revered blue pencil was first sharpened.

It seemed an appropriate tribute to Arthur Seldon's work to assemble a collection of essays from among the most dis-tinguished victims of that pencil. My initial hope was that the ten outstanding economists whose work appears here would submit essays on their specialist topics so as to build up a serviceable guide to what has been called (despite its venerable origins) 'the New Economics', with a Prologue from the man who has shared most in Arthur's work. But, as Arthur would have predicted after years of arguing that planning is fallible, our plans went agley.

Nevertheless, what has emerged is a wide-ranging and provocative survey of many of the most important strands in current free-market thinking. Although the Institute's constitution requires that its Directors, Trustees and Advisers formally dissociate themselves from the conclusions of the authors, it offers this collection of essays as a perceptive contribution to the understanding of some of the most intractable problems of political economy facing the liberal economies of the West—and as a tribute to a much-loved colleague and a ceaseless champion of individual freedom, responsibility and dignity.

April 1986   MARTIN J. ANDERSON

PROLOGUE
Seldon Man

Ralph Harris

Ralph Harris

RALPH HARRIS was born in 1924 and educated at Tottenham Grammar School and Queens' College, Cambridge. He was Lecturer in Political Economy at St Andrews University, 1949-56, and has been General Director of the Institute of Economic Affairs since 1957. He wrote (with Arthur Seldon) *Hire Purchase in a Free Society, Advertising in a Free Society, Choice in Welfare,* etc., for the IEA. His essay, 'In Place of Incomes Policy', was published in *Catch '76 . . .?* (1976). His most recent works written with Arthur Seldon are *Pricing or Taxing?* (1976), *Not from Benevolence . . .* (1977), and *Over-ruled on Welfare* (1979); he contributed the Epilogue, 'Can Confrontation be Avoided?', to *The Coming Confrontation* (1978); and his most recent IEA titles are *The End of Government . . .?* (1980), (with Arthur Seldon) *Shoppers' Choice* (1983), and *No, Minister!* (1985).

He is a Trustee of the Wincott Foundation and a member of the Political Economy Club, former President of the Mont Pèlèrin Society, and a Council Member of the University of Buckingham.

Ralph Harris was created a Life Peer in July 1979 as Lord Harris of High Cross.

2

Seldon Man

RALPH HARRIS

HAVING worked with Arthur Seldon for almost 30 years, I have never ceased to be struck by his penetrating critique of conventional wisdom, however apparently venerable. A good example was provided when I invited his approval of the 1983 Griffiths report on the future management of the NHS. Mr (now Sir) Roy Griffiths was, after all, widely acclaimed as the managing director of the leading grocery chain of Sainsburys. If anyone could devise a structure of command and accountability to secure value for money from £9 billions of annual spending on the hospital service alone, surely he and his three high-powered business associates might have some lessons to teach the medico-union dominated bureaucracy?

Price-less nonsense

I recall my colleague impatiently waving the report aside as unworthy of weighty discussion. Of course, he acknowledged, yet another upheaval of the NHS might check some of the predictable syndicalist deficiencies of the cosy consensus management imposed by the last re-organisation. But even if the apparatchiks would tolerate the proposed appointment of independent managers,[1] the re-organised NHS would still lack both criteria for measuring patient-customer satisfaction and incentives to galvanise the 'public servant'-worker. Thus suppose we had a national food service (NFS) and Mr Griffiths'

---

[1] It would not have surprised Arthur Seldon to read a few months later of ministerial disappointment that the new-found managers of the 14 English regional health authorities were mostly appointed from NHS insiders and promptly paid higher salaries.

grocery shops offered 'essential' foods without direct charge. Instead of queues at the pay desks on the way out, you would have a rush of shoppers arriving to fill their trolleys and push them straight out to load-up their car boots. Mr Griffiths and his accountants might succeed in totting up the bill and getting full re-imbursement of costs from government funds. But how could such a *price-less* Sainsburys maintain its famous efficiency, much less boast of satisfying the consumer better than its competitors, when they would all be like hospitals, part of a supposedly[2] uniform national service?

In such a vivid, direct, persuasive way has Arthur Seldon always applied the basic tool-kit of market analysis to demonstrate the incurable shortcomings—his word might be 'deformities'—of state supply at zero price, along with such other popular phantoms as 'equal service for all' and 'the envy of the world'. There are few economists I have ever met who display so firm and stubborn a grasp of what Lionel (later Lord) Robbins, among his teachers at the LSE, once called 'the more elementary platitudes of the subject'.[3] I would go further and say there is no contemporary economist who has put such 'invincible truisms' (Robbins again) to better use in spreading illumination more widely on major issues of public policy. Thus he traces the root of the weakness of much welfare policy to the failure to understand the difference between the 'income effect' and the 'price effect' of subsidies. When government provides services at low or nil price, it has the beneficial effect of increasing the real income of poorer recipients; but at the same time it removes for everyone the price incentive to economise in the consumption of the services by obscuring their 'opportunity cost' in terms of resources diverted from alternative uses.

It would be impossible to do full justice to Arthur Seldon's contribution to economic education in the years after the Second World War. It runs beyond Britain to America, Europe and Australia, and wider than teachers and students of econ-

---

[2] Of course, the boast of a 'national service' does not in practice guarantee uniformity of even minimum standards, as we have seen from the wide discrepancies in local schools and hospitals.

[3] *The Economist in the Twentieth Century*, Macmillan, 1954, p. 8.

omics to politicians, journalists and businessmen. By his powerful exposition he has made accessible to laymen that which some
professional economists prefer to make inaccessible even to
most of their colleagues. Through what might be called his
'hands-on' policy as the incomparable editorial director at the
IEA, he has liberally multiplied the effectiveness of many of
our authors who, unlike Molière's M. Jourdain, were swiftly
to learn they had not previously been talking (or writing)
acceptable prose.

Blood-money

From the time he wrote *Pensions in a Free Society* in 1957 as the
first publication of the infant IEA, Arthur Seldon has devoted
the larger part of his extensive writings to exposing the flaws
of the welfare state. It is almost 20 years since he wrote *After
the NHS*[4] and he has never since tired of predicting its eventual
supercession by a more rational division of labour between
public and private provision of medical care, as of education
and pensions. About the same time, as editorial director, he
commissioned two economists from York to analyse the alternative methods of collecting blood supplies for transfusion through
voluntary donors rewarded by a cup of tea, as in Britain, or
through paying donors a fee per pint of blood given, as in
America and other countries.

The origin of this instructive Paper, it can now be told,
goes back to 1965 when Arthur Seldon was dangerously ill
in hospital for want of a blood transfusion. For a short time
our best hopes of his recovery appeared to rest on the prayers
of the nursing nuns in the Catholic hospital to which he had
been driven by the absence of a private bed in an NHS hospital.
After the necessary supply of blood had been collected just
in time for a successful transfusion, the surgeon admitted that
occasional emergencies stretched the resources of the voluntary
donor system, but added that he hoped Britain would never
find it necessary to pay for blood as in other countries. As
Arthur Seldon told me at visiting time the following day,
his strength had sufficiently returned for him to slap the

---

[4] Occasional Paper 21, IEA, 1968.

counterpane and ask: 'Would you rather a patient died before you contemplate using the market?' The Hobart Paper thus inspired was published in a bright red cover and entitled *The Price of Blood*![5]

Charge for choice

It is no exaggeration to say that the guiding light in his sustained, scholarly campaign for 'choice in welfare' (to quote another IEA title which we wrote together in three editions) has been respect for the well-being and dignity of ordinary individuals whether as patients, students, tenants, pensioners. He has never concealed but rather revelled in the humble origins from which he made his way through state schools and a scholarship to university. Once he had sampled the advantages of private schools for his children and health insurance for his family, he became more impatient to remove the obstacles to others enjoying a similar choice. He has been known to be moved to unscholarly expressions of contempt for politicians in all parties who themselves enjoy choice of private welfare services whilst daring to pretend that state provision will (ever) give lesser mortals what is best (or good enough) for them.

His sustained critique of universal state welfare does not deny an indispensable role for government finance and national minimum standards. Indeed, the merit of selective assistance is that limited tax funds can thereby be more generously concentrated on the minority in genuine need rather than dispersed more thinly over everyone. But state *finance* and state *standards* are not necessarily linked to state *provision*. Hospitals, schools, universities, pensions do not have to be provided by party politicians dressed up as public benefactors, just as the existence of poverty does not require the state to establish a monopoly chain of 'free' bakers and butchers. All that is necessary is for government to top-up low incomes so that the poor can join the rich in spending and choosing for themselves between the varied offerings of the competitive market. Hence the consistent

[5] Michael Cooper and Anthony Culyer, Hobart Paper 41, IEA, 1968.

support he has given for a reverse income tax, educational vouchers, loans for students and portable housing allowances.

As readers of his vigorous academic polemic, *Charge*,[6] will recall, market pricing is far from being the arid concoction of economic theory reproduced in many formal textbooks. Pricing is brought to life in *Charge* as 'neutral . . . useful . . . pacific . . .'. It is 'knowledge . . . a teacher . . . unavoidable' (as we see in the growth of 'black markets'). Price is not a barrier, as uncomprehending sociologists have complained, but 'a link', the indispensable link between buyer and seller. To the predictable battle-cry of 'market failure' this defender of the market was among the first to raise the devastating rejoinder of 'government failure'.

The hidden cost of state welfare

Under the heading of 'the missing link', our tireless mentor hammers home that it is the suppression of market pricing in education (since 1870), housing (since 1915) and medical care (since 1948) which has increasingly plagued these services in a period when higher standards of living, eating, motoring, holidaying and the rest, have been spread by competition in the market-place. It is not merely that the suspension or distortion of prices in monopoly welfare services inevitably reduces output by wasting and misdirecting resources; above all it prevents output being shaped by the varied preferences of individual consumers as pupils, parents, tenants, patients. In *Wither the Welfare State*,[7] he shows that the largest long-run cost of the welfare state is its suppression of the voluntary, mutual and commercial welfare services that had been developing spontaneously since the 19th century.

His indictment of state welfare is by no means completed with such a substantial catalogue of defects. Our champion of choice exposes the further mischief of describing medical care and education as 'free' when most families have come to pay more in tax than the total cost of what they get back from state welfare. Politicians are not simply, mostly engaged in

[6] Temple Smith, London, 1977.

[7] Occasional Paper 60, IEA, 1981.

'carrying coals to Newcastle'; they are purveying fuels the public would not choose for themselves and making the supposed beneficiaries pay through the nose for the privilege. Thus does 'free' welfare deny freedom of choice. And when spreading prosperity would enable more families to choose private schooling or medical insurance, most are prevented by the burden of tax levied for the state welfare services they wish to reject. Most people are prisoners of state welfare because they cannot afford to pay twice for choice in the market. Furthermore, so long as spending on education and medical care is limited to what Chancellors can extort in taxation, so long will both these large components of the service sector be held back from the expansion people would voluntarily finance by direct payment for themselves and their families.

Politically impossible?

What has made Arthur Seldon persevere against all discouragements over three decades in putting the case for choice in welfare?[8] In the first place, he is driven by intellectual probity to stick to his last. But there is also his buoyant faith in the strength of the often-unexpressed urge among prosperous working parents to liberate their families from the insensitive, paternalistic, choice-denying and, therefore, inhumane apparatus of state-provided, tax-financed, bureaucratically-administered, politicised welfare. Why then do not more of the sovereign people respond to the beckoning opportunity of being able to shop around for their doctors, surgeons, hospital beds, teachers, schools, as for their kitchen equipment, garden furniture, videos, music centres, cars, packaged tours? Of course, high taxes reduce most people to dependence upon the state. But why don't the voters encourage politicians to offer alternative policies on welfare that would permit contracting-out of state services or would enfranchise all with choice by direct payment and lower taxes, or through the

---

[8] A complete explanation of his remarkable perseverance would have to pay tribute to the quite exceptional role of his wife Marjorie, whose active, daily encouragement goes far beyond the untiring campaign in support of the education voucher for which she is justly famous in her own right.

ingenious intermediary of the earmarked voucher for education and even for medical insurance?

It was when Arthur Seldon first encountered the 'public choice' analysis of Buchanan and Tullock that he began to shape up to the formidable obstacle of the politicians who have been able to buy votes by appeasing enough sectional interest-groups to get themselves elected. If he has not committed himself to the American solution of imposing limits on governmental discretion by a written constitution, he has advocated the Swiss referendum and citizens' initiative as ways of isolating producer pressure-groups and harnessing widely-dispersed electoral support for more enlightened reforms. Thus from his earliest days as editorial director he instructed IEA authors to follow their analysis through to the framing of proposals for policy without deference to what might be thought at the moment 'politically impossible'. In the first place, he insisted, the economist is unqualified to judge such politically self-seeking calculations. And, secondly, men of ideas should heed Hayek's precept of developing their best argument in the hope of making politically possible that which can be shown to be economically desirable. How we rejoiced together in 1979 when Sir Geoffrey Howe as Chancellor confounded the faint-hearts by sweeping away exchange controls which looked set to last forever![9]

Breadth of interests

The contributions thoughtfully assembled in this volume by Martin Anderson bear testimony to the breadth of Arthur Seldon's interests and associations. In addition to original essays by Professors Buchanan and Tullock as founding fathers of the seminal economic analysis of politics, there are character-istic samples of his preferred micro-economics by his close friends, Professors Yamey and Hutt. As evidence that micro-analysis can provide a sound foundation for macro-economics and modelling, Professors Minford and Walters have offered their own distinctive illumination. The instructive essay on

---

[9] It was all the more a matter for satisfaction that the Chancellor took this step four months after the IEA published *Exchange Control for Ever?* by John B. Wood and Robert Miller, Research Monograph 33, February 1979.

Sir Arnold Plant by Professor Coase recalls, respectively, a leading teacher and famous fellow-student of Arthur Seldon's at the LSE half-a-century ago. Professor Kirzner's essay marks the recent revival of interest, led not least by the IEA's editorial director, in the Austrian school of price and market theory.

No collection of essays in honour of Arthur Seldon would be complete without contributions from Professors Hayek and Friedman. In their different, indeed, often contrasting ways, through their writings and personal friendship, both have long provided him with continuing stimulation, encouragement and, I would dare say, inspiration.

One example of Arthur Seldon's editorial fastidiousness has been his gentle but firm chiding of authors (however elevated) for the use of hyperbole, as in the misplaced use of such words as 'unique'. I would, nevertheless, risk so describing his exceptionally wide grasp of serviceable theory allied to fresh, vigorous, vivid prose. On the first attribute I would refer doubters to the invaluable *Everyman's Dictionary of Economics*,[10] which he wrote with his old friend Fred Pennance, whose loss we still mourn. On his incomparable clarity of exposition, the evidence is there for all to savour in more than 20 IEA publications that bear his name as author or contributor, to say nothing of the Prefaces with which he brought to life more than 200 other Papers he produced during 25 years as editorial director.

Seldon man

His unwavering consistency of educational purpose has owed something to the scrupulous avoidance of party political allegiance after his brief student flirtation with the extreme Left gave way to a disillusioning period as an active member of the Liberal Party which he found increasingly illiberal. For a short interval his hopes focused on Mr Heath as the Conservative leader apparently committed to the radical 'Selsdon programme'[11] of tax reduction and economic liberation.

---

[10] First published in 1965 by J. M. Dent, with an enlarged second edition in 1975.

[11] Named after what *The Times* called a 'council of war' by the Tory shadow cabinet at the Selsdon Park Hotel near Croydon, in February 1970, before the June election which made Edward Heath prime minister.

However temporary the rule of 'Selsdon man' before the famous U-turn of 1972, all adherents of the free society must rejoice that 'Seldon man' has proved more durable. At 70, after his first five years of fully-active 'retirement', Arthur Seldon shows no sign of slackening intellectual or physical vigour. May he long continue to encourage, to instruct and, occasionally, to chide us all.

Wanted: New Public-Choice Theories

Gordon Tullock

Gordon Tullock

GORDON TULLOCK is Holbert R. Harris University Professor at the Center for the Study of Public Choice at George Mason University, Fairfax, Virginia (previously based at the Virginia Polytechnic Institute, Blacksburg). He formerly taught at the Universities of South Carolina, 1959-62, Virginia, 1962-67, and Rice, 1967-68. He is editor of *Public Choice*, and author of numerous works including *The Politics of Bureaucracy* (1965) and *Private Wants, Public Means* (1970). For the IEA he wrote *The Vote Motive* (1976), and contributed to three IEA seminars/symposia: 'The Charity of the Uncharitable' in *The Economics of Charity* (1974); 'Bureaucracy and the Growth of Government' in *The Taming of Government* (1979); (with James Buchanan) 'An American Perspective: From "Markets Work" to Public Choice' in *The Emerging Consensus . . .?* (1981).

Wanted: New Public-Choice Theories

GORDON TULLOCK

ARTHUR SELDON used to attend the meetings of the European Public Choice Society; recently he has usually skipped them. He explained that the papers had become too mathematical. Although his explanation is true, I think this was a polite evasion of the real reason: he simply felt that these conferences are becoming less and less interesting.

Unfortunately, if my diagnosis of his motives is correct, I am compelled to agree with him. I do not feel that the Public Choice meetings are less interesting than the standard economic and political science conferences; indeed, I think there is no doubt that they are markedly more interesting. The papers read there are both more technically competent and more deeply significant. But it is true that they are less interesting than they used to be. The rate of progress has decreased.

Revolutionary approach—and results

Public choice started as a revolutionary approach to the age-old problems of politics. Further, in the early days, not only was the approach revolutionary, but the results themselves could be regarded as revolutionary. A new and deeper understanding of what actually goes on in government was clearly achieved. Elaborate theories turned out to generate testable hypotheses. When tested, the hypotheses were in general confirmed. As a result, public choice was a fascinating field in which new and original ideas were frequent.

It was no doubt to be expected, but nevertheless disappointing, that public choice moved from this revolutionary period into a period of consolidation. We still make progress, the papers given at our meetings normally generate new information which is more important than that revealed in the papers in most of the standard economic or political science society meetings, but progress has become relatively slow. In Professor Thomas Kuhn's terms, we earlier went through a 'paradigm shift' and are now in a period of 'normal science'. It is understandable that Arthur Seldon, like me, finds this less interesting than the earlier period.

The history of any field of knowledge is not one of continuous revolutions. Periods of consolidation and regular growth contribute most of the history of science. Sharp, revolutionary improvements are the exception. The revolutionary periods are, nevertheless, the exciting ones. It is my theme here that we need a new revolution—or perhaps several new revolutions—in public choice.[1] It is clearly worthwhile to continue improving what we now know, even if the improvement is unexciting. But we should continuously concern ourselves with the major unsolved problems we face.

Unsolved mystery

Take but one example which, to me at least, is a mystery. In the 19th century, one of the standard arguments for democracy, as opposed to despotic government, was that it tended to be fiscally responsible. This assertion remained true up to about 1960. Democracies would borrow money in time of war or other emergency, but they had balanced budgets most of the time and, indeed, frequently paid off their war debts in inter-war periods.

Beginning in the 1960s, most of the democracies began running large peacetime deficits. The United States, it is true, was involved in a war,[2] but the rest of the democracies were peaceful and prosperous at the time they began deficit financing on a large scale. Although the size of the American economy makes the US deficit very conspicuous, as a share of GNP it is in no way outstanding. Further, American governments were not the pioneers in this new move to deficit financing. Com-

---

[1] I don't deny that it would be nice to have revolutions in economics, or for that matter in physics, too. But my subject here is public choice.

[2] Two wars in truth: there was also the 'war on poverty' which proved more expensive than Vietnam.

pared with Belgium and Italy, their achievements in this field are decidedly modest.[3]

Why this change in behaviour? As far as I know, nobody has any real, well-tested, theory to explain it. Note that it is fairly easy to offer a 'rent-seeking' theory[4] as to why democracies in general would run deficits. But such a theory cannot account for the long period in which democracies did not run deficits. We need a theoretical explanation which covers both periods. There must have been some change in the 1960s.

Choice of explanation

There are, so far as I know, three possible candidates for such a theory. One was invented by my colleague, Professor James Buchanan, one by Congressman Richard Armey of Texas,[5] and the last by myself. There may be others which have not yet been brought to my attention. All of these potential explanations are hard to test, and I cannot say they have been demolished by existing data. But they do have weaknesses when compared with the real world.

All three theories are based on the impact of ideas on government. Armey explains it in terms of the baneful impact of Galbraith's book, *The Affluent Society*.[6] Buchanan puts it down to a long-delayed response to another book, *The General Theory* of John Maynard Keynes.[7] My theory is slightly more complicated and assumes that politicians learned from experience,

---

[3] Belgian deficits have averaged about 13 per cent of GNP in the 1980s, and Italian ones about 15 per cent. Moreover, and as an illustration of how bad information flows sometimes are, American officials apparently are perfectly willing to let central bankers from countries like Italy and Belgium criticise them for running large deficits without the Americans' referring to the larger deficits being run by their opposite numbers in Europe. As a group, the countries who criticise the USA have deficits that are larger than the American deficit.

[4] Professor Hutt's essay (pp. 41-63) discusses 'rent-seeking' (the attempt by individuals or groups to earn returns on effort, capital, etc., larger than those which could be expected in the market) in terms of the exercise of power by trade unions and other organised groups.—ED.

[5] A former Professor of Economics at Texas A & M University.

[6] Hamish Hamilton, London, 1958; Penguin Books, 1962.

[7] Macmillan, London, 1936.

as explained in more detail below. All three theories, in essence, assume that change was not in the real world but in behaviour, as a result of changes within the minds of policy-makers. Obviously, such an hypothesis is hard to test.

Galbraith the culprit?

Let me take up these theories in alphabetical order, beginning with Congressman Armey's. It is certainly true that Galbraith's book, *The Affluent Society*, was immensely influential. It is also true that it came at about the right time to explain the phenomenon. But there are two problems. First, most economists tend to think of *The Affluent Society* as a very minor product compared with the Keynesian *General Theory*, which is the root of Professor Buchanan's explanation. Thus the question of whether Galbraith's book was as influential on policy as would be necessary to create this gigantic change in behaviour is at least an open one. But secondly, and in many ways more importantly, *The Affluent Society* recommended not only increasing government expenditures but also rising taxes to pay for them, specifically a tax on sales. (Earlier in his life Galbraith had been in favour of deficit financing, but that was not the message of *The Affluent Society*.)

Even with respect to government expenditures, the influence of Galbraith is a little hard to identify. The United States began expansion of the share of Federal government in the GNP around 1900. It more or less stopped that expansion about the time when Galbraith's book came out. A number of other countries, of course, expanded their government very sharply after the appearance of *The Affluent Society*, but one would have expected it to influence the USA before other countries. In any event, as far as expansion of the Federal sector was concerned, it can have had little influence in the USA.

Congressman Armey could respond to these comments by pointing out that, although the total Federal share of GNP has not increased particularly since the publication of Galbraith's book, that part of the GNP devoted to non-military matters has, and that Galbraith was in favour of expanding it while contracting the military budget. But this argument does not explain the deficit. Moreover, I find it difficult to believe that *The Affluent Society* was all that influential—which perhaps indicates simply that I think it is a very poor book.

What about Keynes?

Let us turn to James Buchanan's theory, which is somewhat more elaborate, but also pins the cause on one man and one book, Keynes's *General Theory*. Buchanan argues that there was an implicit constitutional rule, probably also thought to be morally important, that the budget should be balanced. This rule restrained politicians who otherwise would always favour borrowing because it lowers the burden on the people who are voting for them now, deferring it to future generations of voters.

If Buchanan is right, the net effect of the Keynesian persuasion was to dissolve this implicit moral check on deficit-financing. By arguing that government should be financed with deficits in periods of depression, Keynes gave the politicians an excuse for doing what they wanted to do anyway. It was not that they began following his advice literally but that his advice corroded a moral principle which they and their voters had previously thought to be binding.

As can be seen, this theory bears some resemblances to Congressman Armey's,[8] but it penetrates more deeply. The Armey theory takes the view that a single author advocated and caused a change in policy. Buchanan's theory is that an author advocated a policy change. Accidentally, and as a by-product, he undermined part of our 'public' morality.

The basic problem with the Buchanan theory is that *The General Theory* was published in 1936, and deficit financing did not begin in earnest until about 30 years later. Further, one would assume that highly Keynesian countries like the United Kingdom would, if this theory were true, have begun deficit financing long before such mildly Keynesian countries as the United States, or such non-Keynesian countries as Japan. As a

---

[8] Perhaps I should put it the other way, since Buchanan produced his theory long before Congressman Armey.

matter of fact, they all began doing it at about the same time. Indeed, the UK was laggardly and is currently one of the few democracies that is not running a relatively large budget deficit, although it is already big enough to cause concern.[9]

In defence of Professor Buchanan's position, it should be pointed out that Herbert Stein, a leading expert on American policy, has taken 1960, and the advent of President Kennedy, as the time when American policy finally became Keynesian. I have never agreed with Stein on this point, feeling that the Keynesian message was absorbed much earlier. But clearly this is an issue on which Stein's authority is more respectable than mine.

Another problem with this theory is that the gradual rise in the deficit reached its high point at a time when the United States was under control of a president who was most emphatically not a Keynesian and when the Senate was also Republican. Further, the Keynesians themselves[10] have in recent years been criticising deficit financing and frequently even say it causes unemployment. How they have reached this conclusion from Keynesian foundations, I cannot imagine.

A third hypothesis

Having gone through two weak theories, I now turn to my own weak theory. This hypothesis is that the development of government deficits is rather like 'going off gold' in the 1930s. The politicians started under the impression that both of these policies, going off the gold standard and running large deficits in peacetime, were literally impossible. Whether by being 'impossible' they meant that there was some kind of law of nature that banned it, or that they thought their voters would vote them out, is unimportant. In spite of both constraints there were first some timid experiments and then the realisation that you could get away with it.

This argument leads to a sort of 'contagion theory'. Further, under this theory, the amount of deficit would tend to rise over time. One country would, more or less by accident, run a

---

[9] There are several special factors which may explain the British case.

[10] With the honourable exception of Professor James Tobin.

deficit which was too large for peacetime; the politicians there would discover that there were no disastrous negative effects, and hence try a little larger deficit the next time. Politicians in the next country, noticing what had happened, would try the same policy themselves. Eventually, of course, limits would be reached.

The weakness of this theory is that it is quite difficult to test. It does carry with it the implication that all of the countries should start at about the same time. But this aspect is not very distinctive. Also, it seems to give a fairly good picture of how politicians actually behave. It seems to fit my general picture of the world better than either the Armey or the Buchanan theory, but that may be personal prejudice.

Better theories required

The theme of my discussion has not been to argue for any of these particular solutions to the problem of the growth of budget deficits. My point is simply that we do not understand what is happening in a very important branch of policy-making. Public-choice theory leads only to vague and untestable guesses.

I do not recommend that economists and political scientists devote all their time to efforts to solve this particular problem; indeed, I think that such efforts would probably be relatively inefficient. What we should do is try to make basic changes in public-choice theory and hope that one of the results explains this particular mystery.

Another area where we have difficulties, which perhaps may underlie the deficit problem, is simply the immense growth of government expenditures in this century. Once again, we have explanations for over-large government expenditures asserting that pressure-groups associated with specific expenditures tend to be fairly small and the costs tend to be dispersed.[11] But this theory, once again, fails to explain why

---

[11]This raises a puzzle that bothered me for a long time. The pressure-groups for specific tax exemptions are also small and the cost is widely dispersed. Indeed, examining the tax code of any modern country will show that such pressure-groups have had a political effect. Nevertheless, it could appear that the expenditure pressure-groups are politically more influential than the tax-loophole pressure-groups. One would expect it to be the other way around.

expenditure took so long to grow. As a share of GNP, American government expenditures changed practically not at all over the 19th century, when the practice of government was certainly as democratic as it is now. In Britain, expenditures went down very sharply. It is particularly notable that this reduction happened in Britain since this was the period of most rapid imperial expansion. Even if the armies sent out around the world may conceivably have been motivated by a desire to exploit the natives, the bulk of their salaries were paid from London. Once again, it seems to me that improvements in the theory are required before we can explain this growth in state expenditure.

Further puzzles

There are numerous other puzzles. To take an old one, the apparent contradiction between the theoretical instability of voting systems[12] and the observed high degree of stability of government in democracies. Policies simply do not change very rapidly. This has been the subject of a long discussion in the journal *Public Choice*, but there seems to be no agreement on the correct solution.

To continue with unsolved puzzles, most public-choice theory is, like most economic theory, based on the assumption of perfect information. No-one believes, of course, that information in either economics or politics is perfect, but it is quite good in economics and this assumption has turned out to work very well.

One of the early discoveries in public choice was that the average voter, if he is rational, will be badly informed unless he happens to pursue politics as a hobby.[13] Any examination of policies will quickly lead to the conclusion that very many policy-makers, and for that matter voters, are making decisions on what appear to be not only false but obviously false

[12]And for that matter dictatorships, as discussed in my forthcoming book, *Autocracy*, Martinus Nijhoff, Dordrecht, Holland.

[13]Even those who pursue it as a hobby tend to be badly informed. They normally are strong backers of one particular party or point of view, which may mean that their information is systematically perverse as opposed to being simply poor.

assumptions about the world. To take a very old economic chestnut, the view that foreign goods pouring into a country cause unemployment, rather than simply switching employment from the industries competing with the imported goods or services to the exporting industries, is very widely held. Indeed, as any economist can testify, it is almost impossible to eradicate this assumption from the minds of students.

The public-choice scholar has no difficulty at all in explaining why people in the textile industries want a protective tariff on textiles. Further, since this group is small and concentrated, and the cost of such a protective tariff would be widely dispersed, we would anticipate that they would tend to be politically successful. But what we cannot explain is why people who are injured by such a protective tariff seem to think that it is a good thing.

These arguments on information do not, strictly speaking, damage public-choice theory; they simply make it rather less useful for the real world. The market, whether political or economic, provides what people want, not what they *should* want. Thus, if consumers of textiles want protective tariffs on textiles because they feel that such restrictions are vital for their own well-being, the economist/public-choice scholar, observing this behaviour, will say that the consumers are misinformed but that the institutional structure will tend to give them what they want. Thus this particular puzzle is not strictly a theoretical problem for public choice, although it is a problem to which I think public-choice analysts should address themselves.

Further progress awaited

Martin Luther King used to give a good speech on the theme that 'We've come a long way, but we've a long way to go'. This is an accurate description of the present status of public choice. There is no doubt that public-choice economists have made major progress. There is equally no doubt that a lot more progress is required. There is also little or no doubt that the really startling and important achievements of public choice were made in its early history and that currently the rate of progress, although faster than in conventional economics, is still much slower than it used to be.

But that we still have a long way to go does not mean that we should not try to apply our present knowledge. We know much that was not known by the people who designed the existing institutions of government, and hence we can suggest significant changes and improvements. At the moment, public choice is a new branch of economics without a large following, and the prospects for making a large impact on policy are not immediately encouraging. Nevertheless, there is every reason to continue pushing in that direction, and we do make progress.

As I argued above, what we require now is further revolutions. But making this claim is a long way from saying that we can produce them. Most current public-choice research is what Kuhn would call 'normal science', operating within existing paradigms, gradually elaborating and verifying the existing theory. Since this is the traditional route for scientific progress, we cannot complain. Further, although I would like a revolution, I have some difficulty in suggesting methods of obtaining it. Perhaps an obscure junior clerk in the Swiss patent office will come to our rescue.[14]

Nevertheless, I do have some suggestions for directions in which I think there is potential for improvement. As the reader may know, I am a strong proponent of experimental methods in the social sciences, even though I rarely run experiments myself. Most experiments so far have been in the classic mould of testing hypotheses. I would like to suggest some barefoot empiricism in these areas. Set up, for example, an experimental voting system with a built-in cycle and see what happens. It should be said here that a number of the voting experiments have operated in circumstances in which a cycle is at least possible and normally they reach a definite, non-cyclical outcome. But as far as I know there has been little effort to determine why this is so. In particular, adjusting the parameters more or less at random, with the intent not of testing a specific hypothesis but simply collecting data on which parameter changes lead to cycles and which eliminate

[14]One of whose predecessors discovered the Theory of Relativity in a tram on his way to work in Bern in 1905.—ED.

them might be a worthwhile activity. If it turns out that cycles are extremely hard to generate despite the mathematical proofs, this outcome would imply that something or other is being left out of the mathematics.

The spread of ideas

But, more importantly—and here we approach fairly directly the kind of work that Arthur Seldon himself has done—we should be interested in the formation and spread of ideas in society. I am not being facetious when I say that the study of women's fashions might be a valuable technique in the development of public choice. On a more homespun ground, the study of the spread of public-choice ideas among economists and political scientists[15] is not only of direct importance but it also provides an opportunity for research.

Here again, Arthur Seldon has been important in both changing the intellectual climate in Britain (and to a lesser extent in the United States) on economic matters and in spreading public-choice ideas. But his methods have been those of a skilled publicist. If he has a formal theory, he has never sent it to *Public Choice*. We urgently require such a theory.[16] It seems likely that it would contain two basic components: an explanation of the process whereby ideas spread, and a discussion of which ideas are most likely to catch on—in other words, the intrinsic 'attractiveness' of an idea, and a spreading mechanism.

Let me take two rather ancient ideas: Christianity and Islam. Christianity spread essentially by missionary activity without government support and, indeed, with intermittent persecution by governments. Its final rise to dominance in the Western world, however, was based on Imperial favour from the time of Constantine.

Islam, on the other hand, seems rarely to have succeeded by any method except military conquest until very recent times. It was Mohammad's army that brought Southern

---

[15]And to at least one member of Congress, Congressman Armey mentioned above.

[16]Arthur Seldon's combination of knowledge of public choice and practical idea-spreading would make him particularly likely to develop such a theory.

Arabia under his control and led to the foundation of Islam. It was the armies of his successors that brought the areas where Arabic is now spoken, together with a number of areas to their east, under the control of the Caliphs. The conversion of the population to Islam from their previous religions was, in general, a gradual process after the military conquest.[17]

What we have here are two different sets of ideas and two different methods of propagation.[18] As far as I know, no public-choice scholar has any idea which of these two methods is better.

These are grand schemes beyond the ken of most governments. But why do we observe the success of Smith, Ricardo and their friends in changing government policy in Britain in the 19th century? Why did their work eventually face reversal in this century? Why was it so hard to spread it elsewhere? Why was Japan an exception to my last generalisation? Why, for that matter, have Arthur Seldon and his colleagues been so successful in effecting a change in the climate of opinion? We have no answers to any of these questions.

In a way, the development of the modern welfare state is simply a revival of what Adam Smith called 'mercantilism', and what most public-choice scholars are apt to refer to as the 'rent-seeking' society, which has been the traditional state of the human race. It is relatively unproductive and leads to widespread poverty, yet it seems to be an attractive set of ideas. For some reason, the consumers of textiles do seem to think that a tariff on textiles benefits them.

But to say that I think the spread of ideas is an important question for investigation and one which we should worry about,[19] does not provide any guidance on how to solve the problem. To some extent, the spread of ideas resembles that of a contagious disease, a point that was emphasised by

---

[17]Indonesia seems to have been converted essentially by missionary activity, and in recent years Islamic missionaries have been very successful in Africa.

[18]I don't imagine that the Christians refrained from use of military force because they wanted to. They simply did not have any.

[19]I have already worried about it to some extent in *Toward a Mathematics of Politics*, University of Michigan Press, Ann Arbor, 1967, pp. 1-18 and 82-144, but I cannot claim that my worry led to any outstanding achievements.

Professor Kenneth Boulding.[20] Unfortunately, this simile is of little help for a variety of reasons, one of which is that the theory of contagious diseases is mathematically intractable even in medical terms. Further, we have little or no knowledge why some ideas seem to spread and others do not. Presumably the media could be dealt with in much the same way as a defective sewage system in the theory of contagious diseases, but even that is of little help.

Voting and the spreading of ideas

To turn to a somewhat more public-choice approach, there seems to be little or no doubt that something resembling voting occurs in the spreading of ideas. I am more likely to believe something if a large number of my friends and acquaintances believe it than if only one or a small minority does. This mechanism, of course, requires that the idea is not one that I will carefully investigate myself, but most political ideas are of that nature. Nor can this approach help us understand the way in which ideas get started, since they must originally be held only by one person, or at least by a very small group.

To say these are difficult problems is not to say that they are insoluble. It is certainly not to say they are unimportant. Further, to repeat what I said above, it is a particularly fitting subject for discussion in connection with the work of Arthur Seldon. Finally, I would emphasise that this is far from a complete list of all the questions on which we would like to be informed and where currently we have no good theory. To repeat Martin Luther King's theme, 'We have come a long way, but we have a long way to go'.

[20]*Conflict and Defense*, Harper, New York, 1962.

Our Times:
Past, Present & Future

James M. Buchanan

James M. Buchanan

JAMES McGILL BUCHANAN has been University Distinguished Professor of Economics and Director of the Center for Study of Public Choice at George Mason University, Fairfax, Virginia (formerly based at the Virginia Polytechnic Institute, Blacksburg) since 1969. Previously he was Professor of Economics at Florida State University, 1951-56, University of Virginia (and Director of the Thomas Jefferson Center for Political Economy), 1956-68, and University of California at Los Angeles, 1968-69.

He is the author of numerous works on aspects of the economics of politics and public choice, including: (with Gordon Tullock) *The Calculus of Consent* (1962), *Public Finance in Democratic Process* (1967), *Demand and Supply of Public Goods* (1968), *Public Principles of Public Debt* (1958), *The Limits of Liberty: Between Anarchy and Leviathan* (1975), (with Richard E. Wagner) *Democracy in Deficit: The Political Legacy of Lord Keynes* (1977), *Freedom in Constitutional Contract* (1978), *What Should Economists Do?* (1979), and (with H. Geoffrey Brennan) *The Power to Tax: Analytical Foundations of a Fiscal Constitution* (1980).

Professor Buchanan is a member of the IEA's Advisory Council. The IEA has published his *The Inconsistencies of the National Health Service* (1965), (with Richard E. Wagner and John Burton) *The Consequences of Mr Keynes* (1978), and (with H. Geoffrey Brennan) *Monopoly in Money and Inflation* (1981). He has also contributed to two IEA seminars/symposia: *The Economics of Politics* (1978) and (with James Buchanan) *The Emerging Consensus . . .?* (1981).

Our Times: Past, Present & Future

JAMES M. BUCHANAN

IN his outstanding *A History of the Modern World*,[1] Paul Johnson dates the start of our era in 1919, the year of my birth. I shall take the licence here of placing Arthur Seldon alongside me, despite a small temporal displacement, and I shall adopt the rubric 'our times' to apply to both of us and to all our temporal peers. I want to examine broadly three periods: first, our past, extending roughly from the end of World War I through to the 1970s; secondly, our present, essentially the decade of the 1980s; and, thirdly, our future, the 1990s and beyond. I shall do so from the only perspective that is possible for me, that of the political economist. I advance no claim to historical scholarship, and I lack the enthusiasm for science fiction that seems to be required to qualify as a futurist. A second obvious forewarning is that my discussion emerges from the context of American political economy although there are surely implications that extend to the United Kingdom and elsewhere.

From centralism to disillusionment in six decades

The six decades that bridge the first and last fifths of this century include the Great Depression, World War II, and the post-war prosperity. Categorised in terms of ideas that describe public attitudes, the period sweeps through disaffection with capitalism, socialist enthusiasm, community co-operation under authority stimulated by the pressures of wartime, Keynesian euphoria for the centrally directed economy, and, finally, both socialist and Keynesian disillusionment. The first four of these sets of ideas provided both the intellectual justification and the underlying political thrust for the massive expansion

[1] Weidenfeld & Nicolson, London, 1983.

in the relative size of the 'public' or governmental sector in the polity-economy, perhaps the single most decisive characteristic of the era considered in the large.

World War II is critical to an understanding of the era because it generated a 'Peacock-Wiseman threshold'[2] of governmental organisation and finance that allowed for the introduction of both socialist experimentation and Keynesian macro-economic management, abetted by the continuing disaffection with capitalism. Disillusionment with the prevailing organisation of society and the policy controlling it emerged only towards the end of these six decades; and there was no shock remotely comparable to that of World War II to facilitate the gradual displacement of the now-institutionalised mechanisms of the state. As a result, the relative size of the government sector was not reduced. Policies encouraging the growth of the welfare state continued to proliferate, despite accumulating evidence of their failure, and Keynesian macro-economic management, once it had effectively destroyed the foundations of fiscal and monetary discipline, was left adrift without anchor against prevailing and sometimes violent political winds.

The 1980s, and failure to restore the market

Our present, the decade of the 1980s, is characterised by the observed failures of new administrations in both the United Kingdom and the United States to exploit effectively the disillusionment with socialism and Keynesianism, despite the anti-*dirigiste* and pro-capitalist rhetoric of government on both sides of the Atlantic, accompanied by genuine ideological attachments to the non-socialist, non-Keynesian, and pro-capitalist alternatives.

What we have learned, or should learn, from both our present and our immediate past is something about the magnitude of the difficulty in generating a shift in direction in the basic organisational structure of the political economy without

---

[2] In *The Growth of Public Expenditure in the United Kingdom* (National Bureau of Economic Research, New York, 1961), Alan Peacock and Jack Wiseman present the thesis that high rates of tax in war-time cross tax-thresholds which then allow post-war spending to remain higher than pre-war.

having to provoke a total breakdown.[3] A return to the Peacock-Wiseman notion of threshold will make matters clear. The stringencies of World War II effected a necessary shift in organisational structure from private to state control. Once the threshold was crossed, the prevalence of the basic socialist idea had relatively little difficulty in preventing any massive post-war realignment toward the genuinely capitalist alternatives; and the dominance, since 1980, of the basic idea of the non-socialist alternative in both the intellectual and the political communities is not, in itself, a sufficiently strong force to overcome institutional rigidities and secure organisational change of any practical significance.

The frustration of the more enthusiastic 'reformers' is perhaps natural, but the temptations to be avoided are, first, the attribution of blame to the political leaders for failure to effect change and, second, the attitude of resignation concerning the very relevance of ideas. Ideas can, and do, matter, and political leaders can, and do, make a difference. But ideas and politicians exist in both time and space. And institutions that constitute a social order, once entrenched, are not readily displaced, turned off, or turned around. As economists, we are taught to think always in terms of margins and, at best, ideas and politicians can make a difference only when such margins of opportunity present themselves.

Our present marks a decade in which there have emerged, in either the United Kingdom or the United States, precious few *new* initiatives for governmental direction, regulation, organisation, and financing that, if brought into existence, could not be readily dislodged or dismantled. The 'turning-off of the engine' of governmental growth and expansion has been the only accomplishment of our present; neither the British nor the US Government has succeeded in 'turning the ship around'. The current expansion of the welfare state that both Britons and Americans are witnessing stems almost exclusively from the built-in features of policies initiated in our

---

[3] Professor Mancur Olson (*The Rise and Decline of Nations*, Yale University Press, New Haven and London, 1982) has argued convincingly that the post-war success of countries like West Germany and Japan is due in large measure to their defeat in World War II and the consequent disappearance of institutional rigidities from their economies.

past—and this expansion may be the source of major difficulty in our future.

Could we realistically have expected more than this 'turning-off' result from the intellectual and political shift that reflects the widespread disillusionment with socialism and Keynesianism? Our present should teach us to be temperate in our expectations about political change.

The 1990s: minimal hope of a minimal state?

I speak of 'our' future, and especially as I have defined it as beyond the 1990s, with some trepidation, but our interests surely extend beyond our own life expectancies.

My brief diagnosis of our past and present suggests that we are doomed to continued frustration if we expect advance towards the libertarian ideal of a minimal protective state in which the massive government economy of our present is dramatically reduced in size, scope and power, and in which the generative forces of the market are allowed much more room to play, thereby ensuring both increased productive performance and economic growth. This is a world that, just possibly, 'might have been', but it is neither the world that is nor the world that we can reasonably predict for our future, not even in the most favourable of our projections.

Care must be taken to distinguish between prediction and prescription. If we stick to prediction, we may be unable to foresee the dismantling of the apparatus that describes the welfare state. No such result emerges from any plausible model of the workings of democratic decision-making. As social scientists, our predictions must, it seems to me, remain pessimistic. These predictions depict an economy-polity in what may be called a quasi-equilibrium, in which the burden of financing redistribution to the unproductive through taxation, the printing of money or creation of debt stifles effort and investment and ensures low, zero or possibly negative rates of growth. This predicted quasi-equilibrium may, in itself, contain socially disequilibrating elements, some of which we may discern already in our present, long before our future is yet upon us. Several such elements are discussed below.

Built-in escalation of welfare-state costs
The welfare state prospered mightily as national economies grew rapidly through the 1960s. But as these economies stagnated in the 1970s, the expansion of the redistributive state reached an impasse. But within the structure of the system there are possibilities or probabilities of expansion in expenditures that operate independently of ordinary political decision (the so-called 'budgetary uncontrollables'). These institutions take several forms. First, several redistributive policies remain essentially open-ended, in that persons may qualify for the receipt of transfer payments by modifications in their own behaviour. By exploiting the available margins, people may, by their own private economising, determine their eligibility for transfer payments.

An example is provided by the US disability scheme, under the broader umbrella of social security. In effect, people are allowed to choose when they go on the disability rolls, almost at will. This example also suggests the difficulty faced by any attempt at corrective reform. In the early 1980s, attempts were made to tighten up eligibility requirements for disability payments. But the US Congress reversed the authorisation for change it had earlier voted itself as soon as implementation became effective and people were denied 'their' payments. And this reversal was taken in the face of near-universal acknowledgement of widespread corruption and abuse under the scheme. Similar examples could readily be provided.

A second institution that guarantees the expansion of expenditure quite independently of political decision is the effect of technology on the cost of government policies. In the United States, this relationship appears most strongly in the state financing of medical services to the elderly. Rapid developments in medical technology ensure that life expectancies can be substantially increased by costly care, and precepts of justice are assumed to require that all potential patients have access to the highest standard of care that is technically possible. The medical bureaucracy compounds the problem since its self-interest is served by the increased spending that new technology appears to justify. Attempts to cap the costs of health-care have failed—with the bureaucrats' blessing.

A third institution that ensures internally-generated patterns of growth in policies that promote welfare redistribution is the divorce of age-related payments from both life-expectancy and relative size of the number of taxpayers. In the early decades of the next century in particular, productive workers in the United States will be saddled with increasingly onerous taxes to finance promised transfers to the aged. This example again offers evidence of the effective political barrier to reform. The mere suggestion of minor adjustment in old-age pensions is considered an act of political suicide in the United States. The old-age-pension system is deemed sacrosanct in the 1980s, despite near-universal agreement that some vulture-sized chickens may come home to roost with a vengeance in the 2000s.

Finally, the observation that in both our present and our near future we are financing significant and growing shares of state expenditure by debt rather than by taxes should give pause to anyone who ponders whether the quasi-equilibrium of our present is sustainable over the long term. Charges levied to service government debt cannot, by the simple logic of compound interest, be allowed to command ever-increasing shares of budgetary outlay.

For these and other reasons, there are at least some characteristics of a time-bomb in the modern welfare state; indeed, my assignment for this essay was put in precisely such terms. But the time-bomb metaphor suggests also that there will be some ultimate explosion, some dramatic collapse of the structure. And it is this element of the time-bomb metaphor that I reject. The set of projections I deem plausible for our future contains no cataclysm. The internal dynamics may be less explosive than mere projection of current trends suggests, and, further, there may yet be political adjustment along some of the margins of potential growth of spending. But any of the developments I can foresee embodies the survival of a financially burdensome and bureaucratically heavy-handed re-distributive sector of state welfare. In our present and near future, we may have approached the limits of this burden, but we are whistling in the wind if we anticipate breakdown and reversal.

The role for political economy

I mentioned earlier the necessity of distinguishing between prediction and prescription, and my discussion of our future (above, p. 34) was almost exclusively predictive in nature. My role as a social scientist must be separated from my possible role as a political economist, whether I adopt or eschew value-judgements. In the predictions above (pp. 34-36), I have implicitly assumed that the socio-economic-political institutions of our present remain roughly in place. As a positive political economist, describing not prescribing, I can try to diagnose the flaws in these institutions of social order that produce what appears to be the welfare-redistribution dilemma of our present and future. Clearly, I cannot here outline the entire branch of political and economic theory we now call 'constitutional political economy', but it may be useful to isolate a single characteristic of our times that goes far towards explaining what we observe in the social order of our present.

As the modern state emerged in this century and became the vehicle for massive transfers of wealth, the political competition for support from organised groups intensified and the criteria for 'success' in politics shifted in favour of people who catered to *short*-term demands. The statesman-politician, who may have occasionally taken a long-term perspective on social problems, was effectively replaced by the career politician who is responsive to organised pressure-groups and has neither an interest in nor a competence for consideration of long-term socio-political viability.

If I briefly diagnose the welfare-redistribution dilemma in this way, when I shift to the role of a normative political economist I am necessarily led to concentrate on the 'rules of the game' that determine the political order of our times. Normative suggestions for policy changes, given an unchanged set of rules, are likely to go unheeded, and, if heeded at all, to affect policy only temporarily.

Arthur Seldon's insight, as a practising political economist, has long embodied the recognition that the 'economics of politics', or 'public choice', warrants careful attention, especially in its emphasis on political rules. He has incorporated public choice into his analytical approach, which has taken his prescriptions for policy beyond more familiar efforts to advance suggestions for piecemeal change within existing rules. Arthur Seldon has also recognised that, despite the depressing evidence that the state will not shrink overnight, there remains an important role for the genuine libertarian, whose dreams may be unreal, but whose vision of a social order may well be necessary to keep those of us who are more pragmatically inclined from resignation and despair. Arthur Seldon has been able, more than most of us, to combine realism in prediction with continued idealism in vision. Our times have been, are, and will be better in consequence.

The 'Power'
of Labour Unions

W. H. Hutt

W. H. Hutt

W. H. HUTT was born in London in 1899 and, after First World War training as a pilot in the RFC and RAF (1917-19), studied at the London School of Economics, where he took the B Com degree. After four years in publishing, he joined the University of Cape Town in February 1928 as Senior Lecturer. In 1931 he was appointed Professor and Dean of the Faculty of Commerce, and later also Director of the Graduate School of Business, which he inaugurated. He was elected Professor Emeritus in 1965.

Visiting Professor of Economics, University of Virginia, 1966; subsequent appointments at Rockford College, Wabash College, Texas A and M University and the Hoover Institution on War, Revolution and Peace, Stanford University (as visiting Research Fellow). From September 1970 to June 1971 he was Distinguished Visiting Professor of Economics, California State College. At present he is Distinguished Visiting Professor of Economics at the University of Dallas.

Professor Hutt has published numerous articles and books. His principal writings are *The Theory of Collective Bargaining* (1930, re-published in the USA, 1954); *Economists and the Public* (1936); *The Theory of Idle Resources* (1939); *Plan for Reconstruction* (1943); *Keynesianism—Retrospect and Prospect* (1963); *The Strike-Threat System* (1973); *A Rehabilitation of Say's Law* (1974). For the IEA he wrote *The Economics of the Colour Bar* (1964); *Politically Impossible . . . ?* (1971); *The Theory of Collective Bargaining 1930-1975* (1975); and contributed 'Immigration Under "Economic Freedom"' to *Economic Issues in Immigration* (1970).

The 'Power' of Labour Unions

W. H. HUTT

'Power' and 'freedom'

In the vocabulary of the social sciences, the term 'power' has meaning only in the context of discussion of human freedom. But 'freedom' is an elusive concept, and consideration of its relation to 'power' raises issues of considerable conceptual complexity. Towards the end of the last century, M. Pantaleoni tried to clear up some of the difficulties in an article entitled 'An Attempt to Analyse the Concepts of "Strong and Weak" in their Economic Connection'.[1] Since the Second World War three eminent scholars have returned to the topic. F. A. Hayek's erudite *The Constitution of Liberty*[2] has much helped us to clarify the issues; while Bertrand de Jouvenel[3] and Helmut Schoeck[4] have treated different aspects of the same problems in a remarkably different manner, but with comparable inspiration and logical rigour. They have reached very similar conclusions on the issues discussed here.

I shall be concerned with the relationship between power and freedom in one of its most important manifestations. The issues are so complex that some reference to the broad question of 'power' in relation to 'freedom' or ('liberty') is required. Some of the complexities are semantic, arising through the use of words in a way which the reader understands perfectly

---

[1] *Economic Journal*, June 1898.

[2] Routledge and Kegan Paul, London/University of Chicago Press, Chicago, 1960.

[3] Bertrand de Jouvenel, *On Power*, Beacon Press (a Beacon Paperback), Boston, 1962; also *Sovereignty: An Inquiry Into the Political Good*, University of Chicago Press, 3rd impression, 1963.

[4] Helmut Schoeck's *Envy* (Secker & Warburg, London/Harcourt, Brace & World, New York, 1969) shows that the urge to abuse power is derived from the very human attribute of envy.

41

well in this context but which are inconsistent with the meaning of the same words in others. 'To be truly free,' said Voltaire, 'that is power'. We all know what he meant. But, generally speaking, the word 'power' implies the existence of a *potential* enemy of freedom, although power itself *may* be the means to freedom.

In this essay the exertion of 'power' will be conceived of as restricting the range of action of an individual, either in the interest of the freedom of all or for the special benefit of some. It will therefore be regarded as infringing that condition of society that we call 'free'.

D. W. Brogan, in his Preface to Bertrand de Jouvenel's book *On Power*, described it as

> 'an argument for repeated stock-taking, for the scrutiny of every new proposal for extending the power of the state or of *any other power-monopolising body*'.[5]

Brogan's phrase seems to me to pinpoint the *practical* philosophic aspect of what may soon come to be accepted as *the* crucial contemporary economic problem. Again in words from Brogan's Preface, de Jouvenel insists on the necessity (from the standpoint of 'freedom') of 'making sure that effective power is not monopolised'.[6]

My concern is with the two related forms of power 'monopolisation' indicated in the passage I have just quoted. The first is what Herbert Spencer was envisaging in the title of his famous tract, 'Man *versus* the State',[7] and what I think we should call 'man *versus* the special-interest group'. My specific concern is with a particular manifestation of power wielded in the second form, namely, by labour unions. But this special problem of the 'monopolisation' of power cannot be fully understood except in the light of a simultaneous awareness of the nature of the power of government. For the authority of the state may be used either to promote or to restrain freedom. Thus, although the principal issue in this essay is abuse of power by monopolistic labour unions, it will be impossible to

[5] *On Power*, p. xv.

[6] *Ibid.*, p. xviii.

[7] Liberty Classics reprint, Indianapolis, Indiana, 1981.

avoid recognising and questioning the authority exercised in a democracy by and through those small groups of private people entrusted with vital functions whom we call 'governments'.

Thus the engrossing of power against which de Jouvenel has warned us concerns the accretion or seizure of the ability to restrain, control or 'exploit' others by (i) a person, (ii) a group, or (iii) a government. Realism compels us to recognise that, in the contemporary world, both legislation and its administration are normally privately motivated and that power has, indeed, been 'monopolised'.[8]

'Exploitation' defined

In the argument that I shall present, a rigorous definition of 'exploitation' may be desired. As I have used it here, it means: any action taken, whether or not through discernible private coercion (collusion), or governmental coercion, or whether through monopolistic or monopsonistic power, which, with a given availability of resources (including the stock of knowledge and skills), reduces the value of the property or income of another person or group of persons, or prevents that value from rising as rapidly as it otherwise would—*unless this effect is brought about through* (*a*) the dissolution of some monopolistic or monopsonistic privilege; or (*b*) the substitution of some cheaper (labour- or capital-saving) method of achieving any objective (including the production and marketing of any output); or (*c*) the expression of a change in consumers' preference; or (*d*) through taxation authorised by explicit legislation accepted as 'legitimate' in any context.

The power of government to make and enforce the rules which all must obey is more often termed 'sovereignty', by which is meant the power which is obeyed in practice, whether or not the 'sovereignty' is defensible. The complexities and dilemmas encountered in attempts to reach conceptual clarity on the implications of 'power' or 'sovereignty' in relation to 'human freedom' led me, in a book published in 1936,[9] to

---

[8] For the sake of simplicity I shall not treat separately the power of a wealthy individual. It corresponds exactly to that of a group.

[9] W. H. Hutt, *Economists and the Public*, Jonathan Cape, 1936, Chapter XV.

insist that we cannot conceive of 'liberty' as a condition in which every person is allowed to 'do as he wishes' or, in today's delightful vernacular, to 'do his own thing'. 'When I can do what I want to do', said Voltaire, 'there is my liberty for me.'[10] But this notion is seriously incomplete; for one person might 'want' to enslave others, intimidate them, or steal from them.

Essential role of consumers' sovereignty

It follows that, for individuals to be free, they must necessarily be subject to some restraints. This requirement applies first to conventional or constitutional restraints on the group of people who have acquired the privileges and duties of the right to rule (i.e., governments). Secondly, it applies to individuals or groups operating in the market—selling, buying, or bartering services (inputs), products (outputs) or resources (assets). The purpose of these restraints is to ensure that one person or group shall not coerce another person or group, except in defence of the freedom of others. And the restraints applied through the market system are 'social'—that is, imposed under the 'democratic' form of what I have called 'consumers' sovereignty'.[11]

Sovereignty in this form can be envisaged as the exercise by people in their role as consumers of their right to buy or refrain from buying ouputs offered, at the prices asked. Consumer choice then determines, *via* 'market signals', the manner in which scarce resources can be profitably used by their owners. The discipline so administered is a legitimate and 'democratic' use of the individual's ability to contribute to the power which directs the employment of assets, including labour.

In 1936, developing these ideas, I emphasised two forms of *legitimate* power or sovereignty: (*a*) *democratic* governmental power, and (*b*) free-market power (i.e., '*democratic* consumers' sovereignty'). Both forms are compatible with that condition

---

[10]Quoted by de Jouvenel, *Sovereignty, op. cit.*, p. 248n.

[11]I believe that I was the first to use this term: *cf.* my *Economists and the Public, op. cit.*, Chapter XVI, and my 'The Concept of Consumers' Sovereignty', *Economic Journal*, 1937.

of the individual which, from the standpoint of the consensus of ethical opinion, would be accepted as 'free' if the issues were understood.

Both governmental and market power can be seen to be essential for the orderly functioning of *any* form of society. But a slave economy and a slave market can operate in an orderly manner. Neither government nor market institutions have to be 'democratic' to be orderly. But to achieve 'freedom' from illegitimate power, it is imperative that both governmental and market controls be 'democratic' in a sense which I shall now explain.

In respect of government, the term 'democratic' does not mean simply that the rulers are chosen by counting votes, and still less universal suffrage ('one man, one vote').[12] Certainly it means that governments can be changed, without violence, through elections. But in a truly 'democratic' society, the discretion of governments must be restrained through 'rules for making rules'. The restraints must have the purpose of preventing either government or market institutions from being used to subject some persons to the will of others. The most usual form in which such subjection occurs is through 'exploitation'—that is, the transfer of income or property from one person or group to another.

The limits to government discretion

Let us consider first the required limitations on government discretion. Freedom, as I conceive of it here, will be achieved if constitutional enactments or strong conventions prevent the people who form governments from using their power for their own personal profit, or for the special benefit of majorities or constituents, or for the private advantage of other electorally influential groups. More positively, a free society can be attained only if governments are allowed to act solely for the collective benefit, legislation being unconstitutional unless it

[12]It may be held that certain groups of people have interests which are incompatible with the right to choose or change rulers. Even so, they can still share in all the benefits of the order and freedom achievable through 'democratic' government. For instance, I have enjoyed these benefits in the United States for over two years, although I have retained a foreign nationality.

is non-discriminatory. Thus freedom precludes as unconstitutional all legislation or executive discretion for the *special* advantage of, say, 'public servants', or the dairy industry, or the plumbers, or the teachers, or the unions, or the medical profession, or the Whites, or the Blacks, or importers, or exporters, or debtors, or creditors, or the rich, or the poor, or men, or women, or the rulers' friends, or contributors to 'campaign expenses', or groups of voters, and so forth.

To ensure that government operates for the collective interest, instead of acting now largely for special interests, its central and local activity must be restricted to such 'classical' tasks as the maintenance of peace (an army and armaments); the administration of police and justice; and the making and application of a framework of non-discriminatory rules under which entrepreneurs, disciplined by the wish to avoid loss and incentives to seek profits, can plan and co-ordinate the achievement of socially-expressed ends.

The rules required cover such diverse fields as the enforcement of contracts (including any contract to maintain a money unit of defined value), weights and measures, traffic regulations, anti-trust, and the kind of activities *supposed* to be undertaken in the USA by agencies like the FDA, the SEC, the FTC, the ICC, the Fed., and the like. But for 'freedom' to be assured, such agencies must be permitted only an interpretative discretion over the laws they administer; and their interpretations must be checked by politically independent courts.

Under representative government the voters have the right to choose and change rulers from time to time. That right *is* an important requirement for human freedom. But alone it does not cause political sovereignty to be effectively vested in 'the people'. We cannot place too much stress on the truth, enunciated by de Jouvenel, that 'Divine Right and Popular Sovereignty, which pass for opposites, stem in reality from the same trunk'.[13] The safeguards of separation of powers—judicial, executive and legislative independence—are insufficient on their own to guarantee that government power will not be misused.

[13]De Jouvenel, *On Power*, p. 27.

Social discipline of the market

I have explained that whether or not governmental power over the individual can be said to be compatible with individual freedom is dependent upon the nature of the discipline imposed on rulers. Very much the same limitations are required for social discipline in the market. The required constraints on the individual in the satisfaction of his consumer preferences are conducive to freedom when they are imposed by an acceptable method of limiting his access to the products of scarce means. That is really what we imply when we use the term 'free market'.[14]

Both consumers and producers are disciplined by competition. Thus each consumer must ultimately compete against all other consumers for the *means* to the ends he seeks.[15] He competes either directly or through entrepreneurial intermediaries. Under the necessary institutional framework, the producer-entrepreneur has an incentive to discover the least-cost method of responding to ends expressed through market signals, and through the incentive to economise he is forced to 'compete', which means that he must attempt to achieve each end he seeks as entrepreneurial intermediary so as to minimise the sacrifice of other ends. His discretion is then limited only in the sense of being restrained by non-discriminatory market pressures. Moreover, through the commands of the free market, he has the strongest motive to use the community's resources for those ends (products) which he forecasts the people will demand. The consumer then enjoys 'liberty' because the same restraints of market-determined values that limit *his* access to the things he may want discipline all other consumers in the same sort of way. Through rationing the distribution of the flow of outputs, the market operates in a non-violent, non-arbitrary way.

The process of competition can be defined as 'the substitution of a lower-cost method of producing and marketing any product or of achieving any objective entailing a sacrifice,

---

[14]The case for government restraint of traffic in drugs, guns, or in pornographic material and the like is, according to the philosophy here explained, the protection of the individual from a form of assault.

[15]All ends to which the required means are scarce are 'products'.

irrespective of the institutional set-up which may be needed to create and/or protect incentives for the process'. And when the institutional framework promotes the incentives to avoid loss and seek profit as far as is practicable, we can call the *consumers' sovereignty* exercised 'democratic'.

In the absence of the over-ruling, *via* government or private monopolistic power, of 'free market' or 'social' discipline, individuals whose 'votes' are most heavily weighted are people whose assets, enterprise, energies and skills earn the most; and that, in turn, means (in the absence of monopolistic or monopsonistic abuse) people who are contributing most to the well-being of others. People as consumers, choosing between ends or 'products', are viewed as *sovereign*, while people in their capacity as producers and entrepreneurs are viewed as choosing means to ends and therefore as *subject*.

Through the operation of consumers' sovereignty, producers are governed by consumers. In a money economy, consumers and producers must, to buy or sell, offer money's worth in one form in order to get money's worth in another. When each consumer has a similar power to command others in their role as producers, we have the 'democratic form' of 'consumers' sovereignty'. Individuals are then constrained through a *social* sovereignty, as distinct from that *private* sovereignty exerted when some right to coerce others is vested in a monopolistic group, or when a government is commanded by special-interest groups. Of course, because private power in practice often overrules social power, consumers' sovereignty is far from perfectly 'democratic'.[16]

To ensure that consumers' sovereignty will be 'democratic' and entrepreneurs truly 'subject', a framework of law and enforcement has to evolve, or be designed, so as to create or protect what I have called the incentives to avoid loss and seek profit. Under the required framework, entrepreneurs are rewarded who are most successful in (i) observing consumers' current preferences, (ii) forecasting their future preferences,

---

[16]That is, the expression of consumers' sovereignty is moulded by special interests which work either through government directly or through government toleration of privately contrived coercion. Even so, consumers' preferences can never be wholly ignored.

and (iii) achieving the least-cost response to them, while entrepreneurs are penalised who (through defective judgement or bad luck) fail in this forecasting and economising role.

My use of the words 'sovereignty' and 'democratic' is, of course, metaphorical. Yet are not those attributes of *state sovereignty* (which, I have suggested, contribute to the freedom of the individual) exactly those which can be so clearly observed in the operation of *consumers' sovereignty* in 'the free market'? If incentives could be released to subject 'the small groups of private people we call "governments" ' to a political discipline as effective as the social discipline I have called 'democratic consumers' sovereignty', the function of governing could then indeed be viewed as 'of the people, for the people, by the people' (if not in the common and naïve connotation of this phrase).

The case against union coercion

Against this background we can at last turn to union power. We are not concerned with the useful services unions can perform, but solely with their organisation of *privately-motivated coercive power*. This power is, in a broad sense, exercised in a two-fold manner.

The first is through intimidation, physical violence and sabotage against competitors, non-strikers, strike-breakers, managements, and even non-union competing firms. This exercise of power occurs because of a *de facto* exemption from the normal sanctions of society against physical violence and sabotage (even if, *de jure*, the outlook has become brighter, in the UK at least).[17]

Secondly, and incomparably more important, is a form of coercion used for the same purposes but which is less commonly regarded as illegitimate—'peaceful coercion' through threats to disrupt the continuity of economic co-operation.

The power of the threat to strike is not only the source of the authority the unions have won to discipline their own willing

---

[17]There is a large literature dealing with coercion of this type. Sylvester Petro's contributions are most important. E. P. Schmidt's *Union Power and the Public Interest* (Nash, Los Angeles, Ca., 1973, especially Chapter 9) is another outstanding analysis and exposure of the consequences.

or unwilling members, but also denies freedom to potential competitors. It is also used, of course, in attempts to exploit investors.[18] At times it is used ruthlessly against third parties— non-parties to the 'dispute' who have, in many countries, been denied the right to sue for damages. But, most importantly, union power is used against the community as a whole, as consumers and producers alike. For the disruption of one set of activities throws into disorder the work and life of others, often in large numbers.[19] Furthermore, the strike is a form of warfare which requires strategy and the maintenance of morale, so that it is essential during peace to keep alive the war spirit: mistrust and hostility towards the employer as 'the enemy'.

Strike-threat 'intolerable infringement of human freedom'

The threat to strike (which Mises called 'the gun under the table') *can* be used for good or noble purposes. Nevertheless, even when the objective is defensible, we are forced to regard all private use of coercive power (whether by boycott or strike) as an intolerable infringement of human freedom. As I insisted in my book, *The Strike-Threat System,*

> 'we should have to condemn the Mafia even if it could be shown that the revenues of racketeering were being used to subsidise opera, cancer research or civil rights movements'.[20]

The strike is a form of private warfare and, as in all warfare, victory is not to the righteous but to the strong. Defenders of strike-threat power are in fact accepting 'might is right!' as a principle.

Yet trade unions typically contend that the workers are forced to strike to secure 'distributive justice'. We must there-fore answer the question: How can the claims of the investors who provide the assets that multiply the yield to human effort

[18]Yet investors have taken the risk of providing the tools of labour—the assets which multiply the yield to human effort. Moreover, investors continuously finance replacement of materials and work-in-progress.

[19]The New York transit strike of 1966 is an apt example. The British coal strike of 1926 was almost as disastrous as the general strike of that year.

[20]W. H. Hutt, *The Strike-Threat System*, Arlington House, New Rochelle, New York, 1973, p. 44.

be balanced against the claims of 'labour' on the value of the product?

In the textbooks of labour economics, the words 'justice' and 'injustice' constantly occur. I cannot recall ever having seen an explicit reference to justice to investors who, as entrepreneurs, forecast the wants of the community and take the risk of providing the assets required to satisfy those wants. And what about justice to consumers? In 1935 a book appeared entitled *Are Trade Unions Obstructive?*.[21] The word 'consumer' occurred once in the Preface but was not used again anywhere in the book.

Moreover, because labour costs imposed by duress reduce profitable outputs and sales, what about justice to workers who are laid off? And can we disregard injustice to those who would otherwise have improved their productivity, earnings and prospects as additional recruits for the activities rendered less profitable? When costs are raised through union power, the prospective returns from employing more labour are reduced so that the incentives to avoid loss force men and assets into inferior, 'sub-optimal' employments.

Of course, the attitude of most opinion-makers (or opinion-followers) in the press, broadcasting, television, churches, schools and politics is that the only relevant ethical consideration stems from their conviction that investors earn too much and the workers too little. But it can be shown that, when potential investors expect labour costs to be exposed to strike-threat coercion, they are unexploitable. There have certainly been periods during which some property transfers from investors to workers have been achieved through union aggression,[22] but that is simply because investors as a whole have failed to predict the extent to which they are exploitable.

---

[21]J. Hilton *et al.*, *Are Trade Unions Obstructive?*, Gollancz, London, 1935.

[22]The notion of transferring property may require explanation. If, through a rise in labour costs imposed by the threat of a strike, the aggregate value of a corporation's shares declines by $£x$, other things equal, the successful unionists will have gained an addition to their income which, when capitalised, will equal $£x$. In practice, the capital transferred is (with unimportant exceptions) treated as income by the unionists who receive it, and consumed.

The calculations made by investors

When investors realistically forecast their vulnerability, they will make full allowance for the probability of union power being used to seize part of their capital. But in assessing the value of assets they can risk in any activity, they will rely on the hope that the unions will not wish to kill the goose that lays the golden eggs, or unduly to harm the goose's fertility. They will rely also upon three *probabilities*. The first is that, although in a society which tolerates strike-threat coercion technological progress will be discouraged, it will not come entirely to an end, so that labour-economising and capital-saving achievements in non-competing fields will steadily be raising the source of demands for most prospective outputs. Secondly, in spite of the depressive effects of the use of union power, aggregate income will continue to increase through continued thrift (provision for the future which normally takes the form of the net accumulation of assets). Thirdly, governments will find it expedient to inflate (reduce the value of the money-unit) which, when this action is unanticipated, will have a wide co-ordinative effect in the short run, since inflation is expected to cause prices to rise ahead of costs.

Investors today expect managements to be expert in avoiding (as far as possible) capitulations to strike-threat pressures, but they know they cannot be certain that the managers will be wholly successful. They know simply that the avoidance of a future capitulation to union power will bring a windfall gain, while capitulation to a particularly heavy wage-demand will bring a windfall loss. Thus, in every decision to retain, replace or provide (accumulated) assets in any productive activity, entrepreneurs who are forecasting rationally must regard the seizures of property referred to earlier as prospective costs which reduce profitable investment in that activity. From the viewpoint of society as a whole, the consequences of union power so used will be that the *composition* of the stock of assets of the community will be adversely affected. In general, the most productive and wage-multiplying types of assets are the least versatile, therefore the most exploitable by unions, and hence most likely to be avoided by investors until exploitation is prohibited. Investment in that form must certainly decline relatively to investment in non-unionised activities or in more versatile—less specialised—resources. The damage to the material well-being of labour as a whole (we are all consumers) is beyond calculation.

A related issue is the prices of assets the accumulation of which has been continuously raising the yield to labour's efforts. The assets used in occupations producing goods with a relatively short economic life span (consumer goods) compete with the assets used in making goods of a relatively long economic lifespan (producer goods). Wage increases imposed by duress, or 'hikes', in the occupations producing consumer goods are in practice matched by similar 'rises', or 'hikes', of wage-rates in producer-good occupations. Now, other things equal, the cheaper the assets required in any activity, the stronger will be the demand they express for the complementary factor: labour—that is, the higher will be the free-market value (through natural scarcity) of the workers' services. Hence, for this reason alone, strike-threat pressures tend to defeat the objective at which the unions claim to be aiming.

I have referred to the likelihood that there have been periods in which capital was widely confiscated through strike-threat power and used as income by the union members. This transfer was probably occurring, for instance, during the years following the Wagner Act of 1935 in the United States. Nevertheless, the most careful empirical studies show that the proportion of income accruing to labour did not increase. As P. Sultan has commented:

> 'It is surprising that at the very moment in history when unions emjoyed tremendous power and influence, the relative wage differential accruing to the union sector should appear to diminish'.[23]

The explanation seems to be that the swollen prospective costs of replacing assets in capital-intensive activities which are, on the whole, most important in the union sector, were reducing the relative profitability of that sector.

---

[23]P. Sultan, *Labor Economics*, Henry Holt (Holt, Reinhart & Winston), New York, 1957, p. 73.

The fallacy of the 'countervailing power' argument

I must now give some attention to the suggestion that union power is 'countervailing power'. It is said that the unorganised worker has 'inferior bargaining power' in the determination of wage-rates unless he can resort to the threat to strike. This fallacy was put very lucidly by a famous judge—Lord Francis Jeffrey—in 1825, very shortly after the repeal of the British Combination Laws:[24]

> 'A single master was at liberty at any time to turn off the whole of his workmen at once—100 or 1,000 in number—if they would not accept the wages he chose to offer. But it was made an offence for the whole of the workmen to leave the master at once if he refused to give the wages they chose to require.'[25]

This sounds, of course, like an intolerable injustice, and so it appeared to the illustrious judge. But that word 'master', like the word 'employer' today, refers in truth to the *residual claimant* (in the 20th century most frequently a corporation) on the value of what is being produced.

Through the managers, who are responsible to their stockholders, decisions about how much to invest in the amount of employment required to produce any commodity or service will be determined by the point at which marginal prospective yields will equal the rate of interest. Just as Molière's *bourgeois gentilhomme* was astonished to be told that he had always spoken prose, so will most managements be surprised when told that they are continuously thinking of the marginal increment when deciding on how much to retain, replace or add to the value of different inputs in different combinations. Yet that *is* what they are doing when they are planning to use the resources at their command to their best advantage. The value the managers will put at risk (i.e., the magnitude of outputs planned) will depend, *inter alia*, upon what they judge they will have to offer in order, first, to attract additional workers

---

[24]Between 1799 and 1825, these laws had aimed at strengthening the ancient common law against restraint of trade, and about forty statutes (applying to particular trades or industries) were enacted against monopolistic pricing and wage-rate fixing.

[25]Quoted in Sidney and Beatrice Webb, *History of Trade Unionism*, 1920 edn., Longmans, London, p. 72.

from their existing employment (which will require a higher offer than the workers' current wage-rates), or from the ranks of the unemployed (which will require wage-rates not lower than those which the unemployed expect to be able to command, sooner or later, if they do not accept the offer); and, secondly, to retain such of their existing employees as they judge can provide profitably priced inputs (labour) at wage-rates at least as high as the workers believe they can command elsewhere (allowing for the costs and inconveniences of movement).

In the absence of monopsonistic (or oligopsonistic) abuse, and provided there is no government restraint on the incentives to avoid loss and seek profit, it will be to the investors' advantage that managers shall attract or retain all workers whose output is expected to be worth more than their costs. And, still under the *assumption* that there is no monopsonistic or oligopsonistic abuse, *a corporation will have no power to influence the wage-rates which it will be to its advantage to offer*, although the purely interpretative discretion of the management in judging what that wage-rate is may well be wrong, in either direction.

Is monopsonistic power a threat to labour?

We now consider the possibility of the abuse of monopsonistic power which we have so far assumed away. To do so fully requires the recognition that it is very easy (where the law allows) to raise the value of inputs and/or outputs by excluding competing resources—men or assets—from an occupation, industry or area. In other words, it is very easy to exploit competitors by acquiring monopsonistic power. But it is very difficult indeed to exploit *complementary or non-competing* factors, such as labour by capital or capital by labour. We have already seen how the flow of capital into non-versatile or otherwise exploitable assets can be reduced by the threat of exploitation.

For similar reasons, labour is unexploitable, unless managements can somehow suppress competing demands for the labour they acquire. The circumstances required for monopsonistic action to reduce wage-rates are those which cause labour to be locked into a firm, occupation, industry or area. This *has* occurred and may occur again. The most obvious case is the 'lock-in contract', under which an employee who leaves a corporation is subject to some penalty, such as loss of pension rights. But if abuses of this kind are important, they are easily remedied. Lock-in contracts can be declared void and illegal except when they are a protection for investment in human capital (like patents to protect investment in research) or the contract is a means of repayment of beneficial loans to the employees, such as removal expenses, and so forth.

Nevertheless, in theory, monopsonistic exploitation of labour is *conceivable*. The most likely way (apart from lock-in contracts) is where, by subtle fraud, workers are inveigled into specialised training for an occupation and then find themselves trapped in it. I know of no practical illustration of such a situation. But if it should occur, it would still not justify the private use of force as 'countervailing power'.

Fortunately, there is one simple test for determining whether strike-threat power has been necessary to counter an exploitation which has forced or maintained the price of labour below its free-market value.[26] The test is whether any workers not presently employed in firms paying the disputed wage-rates would be prepared to accept work of the same quality and quantity for lower wage-rates. But after nearly half a century of interest in this subject, I have discovered no case-studies in which proof of previous monopsonistic exploitation has been demonstrated in this way. Only if, at the increased wage-rate, or at any lower wage-rate offered, no firm could recruit additional labour if it wanted to is there evidence of any previous monopsonistic exploitation.

Nevertheless, this problem has been discussed at considerable length by pure theorists, as well as labour economists, during the last three decades. I have therefore tried elsewhere[27] to consider such objections as I have found to the thesis that it is virtually impossible to exploit *complementary* (as distinct from competing) parties.

Oligopsonistic exploitation is rather different in some ways.

---

[26]I.e., below the wage-rates which would be determined in the light of wage-rates in alternative employments open to the workers concerned.

[27]Hutt, *The Strike-Threat System*, *op. cit.*, Chapters 8-9.

But for most purposes it can be regarded simply as a much weaker form of monopsony. In practice, effective exploitation of any kind seems to require iron-clad agreements among employers, secret when vigilant anti-trust is present, that can be enforced by explicit restraints on consumers' individual demands for, or producers' supplies of, outputs. Effective monopsonies must, it seems, rely on penalties.

It is very easy to mistake ordinary entrepreneurial caution in bidding up the value of inputs as collusion by employers in oligopsony. In reality, I suggest, the caution so misinterpreted is nothing more than a realistic representation of Walras's 'groping' process, which he described (badly) as 'the mechanism of competition'.[28]

Allegations of examples of either oligopsony or monopsony always seem rather unconvincing. Thus, there have been allegations of secret 'no poaching' or 'hands-off' agreements on the recruitment of highly specialised and skilled craftsmen, or of executives. But they all imply known conduct of clear illegality under the anti-trust laws. Yet I cannot recall any prosecutions for such reasons in the United States. Can the problem then be of any importance?

Among the many misconceptions on this issue, I shall take the example of areas that are isolated from others by distance and physical barriers. The costs of geographical mobility are therefore high. But this does *not* facilitate the exploitation of labour within the area unless the barriers are man-made. The general principle, which I have explained elsewhere, is that, unless labour is somehow 'shut in' by managements,

> 'within any area sheltered by economic distance, by human inertias and by union-imposed restraints on mobility, the flow of wages will be highest and the distribution of the flow most equal and equitable, when every wage-rate is fixed at the lowest level necessary to retain and attract labour for every activity judged to be profitable'.[29]

And on this issue, we should consider whether it is not true that all *man-made* obstacles to the mobility of labour between

[28]Léon Walras, *Elements of Pure Economics* (AER translation), Irwin, Homewood, Ill., 1954, p. 86.

[29]Hutt, *The Strike-Threat System, op. cit.,* p. 103.

occupations, industries and areas are the consequence of strike-threat power or the lobby power of trade unions.

In spite of the strong probability that monopsonistic exploitation of labour is of minimal importance, apologists are bound to feel that it could occur in particular circumstances, so that the call for some countervailing power remains. Even, so strike-threat power would not be an acceptable countervailing force.

What *can* be done is to bring monopsonistic exploitation explicitly within the scope of anti-trust. Unions could then assume responsibility for the initiation of proceedings against observable collusive monopsony where they believe it is damaging to their members. And the unions could also take the initiative against non-contractual lock-in practices which can be shown to be harmful to their members.

Regressive effects of strike-threat power

We can now consider the regressive effects of strike-threat power. When wage-rates are raised by privately-motivated coercion, the burdensome effects must almost universally be borne by individuals in proportion to their poverty.

Consider first the consequences upon the community as consumers. The following illustration has proved useful in explaining what happens. If the price of leather rises, the prices of footwear products will rise.[30] If the price of labour producing footwear rises, the prices of footwear will rise for the same reason—because, in general, output prices are determined by marginal cost. The circumstances in which these consequences do not follow are unimportant. The effects are obviously regressive.

The sheer arbitrariness of such consumer exploitation ought to be enough to cause universal condemnation of the use of strike-threat power. Thus, workers making products confronted with inelastic demands have a differential advantage because consumer exploitation is facilitated. Nearly all labour economists admit that inelastic demand for the product constitutes an advantage for labour in collective bargaining; but

[30]Because reduced outputs will be profitable.

we will look in vain for any condemnation of the resulting injustice and arbitrariness of the exploitation envisaged.

And what are the consequences upon the wage-earning classes of higher labour costs imposed by duress? As we noticed earlier, a regressive effect is brought about as profitable outputs are reduced in two ways. First, there are lay-offs which drive the displaced workers into less well-paid, 'sub-optimal' employment, or into unemployment when it is collectively 'purchased' through transfers of income (for example, unemployment compensation not based upon actuarially sound insurance). Secondly, there is the exclusion of those who could have improved their earnings, and prospects of earnings, by entering the protected employment, if competition and market freedom had been allowed to influence labour costs.

The most important freedom denied through union power is the right of every individual to accept any employment which he believes will improve his earnings and prospects. The 'closed shop' or the 'union shop' inflicted on managements in so many parts of the world must appear to detached students not only flagrantly regressive but an intolerable negation of individual freedom.[31] Yet even under so-called 'right to work laws', union power can force managements to deny the right of those persons who are, in effect, raising their contributions to the common pool of income from pursuing their wishes. Juveniles and the less fortunate adults, and especially people initially less well qualified or who belong to what Professor Harold Demsetz has called 'non-preferred groups' (e.g., Blacks, non-Whites, Jews, ugly women, elderly women, etc.), can be prevented by various subterfuges (like colour bars, demarcation obstacles, apprenticeship barriers, occupational licensing and—most effective of all—enforcement of 'the rate for the job'[32]) from

---

[31]The sceptical reader might ponder Adam Smith's magisterial verdict on the denial of workers' rights:

'The property which every man has in his own labour, as it is the original foundation of all other property, so it is the most sacred and inviolable. . . . to hinder him from employing this strength and dexterity in what manner he thinks proper without injury to his neighbour is a plain violation of this most sacred property.' (*The Wealth of Nations*, Vol. 1, Ch. X, Pt. II, p. 136 (Cannan edn.))

[32]Sometimes called 'equal pay for equal work', 'the standard rate', or 'comparable work'.

improving their earnings and prospects of earning. Hence if by 'union power' we mean the ability to coerce managements through the threat of organised disruption, its use may enable potential strikers to engross for themselves the ability to achieve skills in, or to become 'attached' to, occupations which would otherwise be open to interlopers. The privileges gained in this way must be balanced against the detriment suffered by people who are debarred from employment at wage-rates which it would otherwise be profitable to offer and which prospective recipients believe could raise their earnings and prospects.

Again, because of the incentive for a union to use power so as not unduly to endanger the employment of its existing members, the strike-threat has been most ruthlessly aimed at industries, or branches of industries, which would otherwise have expanded most rapidly. Unions appear in practice to be little concerned about their demands hampering the growth of their industry, and they seem to be unaware of or to ignore their suppression of countless better-paid openings for less-privileged workers which would have been available through demands generated in growing outputs in a free labour market. Moreover, the composition of the stock of skills and the workers' familiarisation and adaptation to the best available outlets for employment must be influenced in a similar manner. After all, the composition of the stock of assets largely determines the composition of the stock of labour. Costs imposed by duress are compatible with 'full employment', but only in 'sub-optimal' activities (for displaced labour).

Damage to capital structure of strike-threat

Many studies critical of the use of strike-threat power em-phasise the enormous social cost of actual strikes, including the loss to the community of outputs and idle plant. But the detri-ment suffered in this form, although obvious and deplorable, is of less importance than the harm inflicted on the structure of capital caused through fear of future strike-threat pressures.

It is often felt that the individual's freedom is infringed because in any firm in which he works he has no voice in the making or administration of the rules to which he is subject.

Elliott J. Berg attributes to such well-known 'labour economists' as J. Dunlop, Clark Kerr, F. Harbison, and C. Myers the view that workers 'live in a state of perennial protest arising from the frustrations implicit in being governed by a web of rules they usually have little to do with making'.[33] But as I have explained, there is nothing to protest about![34] There is no legal, nor any other, barrier to the workers' taking most of the risks, by accepting the residual share, if they so wish. They will then automatically have the right to make and administer all the rules under which they work, appoint all the managers, hire all the assets, and borrow all the circulating capital required. In that case, their earnings will be wages *plus* profits or *minus* losses, just as the investors' earnings are interest *plus* profits or *minus* losses.

The workers will then sacrifice the security of earnings and employment continuity which the wage system provides. It would, of course, entail an inappropriate division of function; for investors can spread their risks over many ventures, while workers who put their future earnings at risk cannot spread risks in that form. A *sharing* of risk and management is, however, by no means out of the question, as I have shown elsewhere.[35] But what is really important is that the rules and their administration by the managers would be unlikely to differ one iota from what they are with investors in the conventional sense taking the residue.

Unfortunately, the word 'employer' suggests subordination to the 'owners'. But the suppliers of the assets and circulating capital are just as subordinate as the workers to the power of consumers' sovereignty. Consumers are the true 'employers'. The assets of a firm are employed just as the workers are. The services of both are embodied in output. The investors willingly submit to the ruthless discipline of the market. Seen from this angle, the investors' acceptance of the residual share from the sale of output is the most important form of social security for the workers that society provides. Our stressing of this

[33]E. W. Bakke, *Unions, Management, and the Public*, Harcourt, Brace and World, New York, 3rd edn., 1967, p. 19.

[34]Hutt, *The Strike-Threat System*, Chapter 6.

[35]*Ibid.*, pp. 80-82.

truth does not of course imply that there is no problem of justice to individuals in the application of social discipline through managerial authority.

Union power is exacted partly through the promise of votes and/or financial support to legislators (central and local) and through general lobbying. The result has been to confer on the unions far-reaching immunities before the law, as well as protection for union members from the competition of the under-privileged. Through minimum wage enactments, 'welfare' hand-outs, occupational licensing, prolonged unproductive schooling and apprenticeship, etc., sectional, private objectives sought through government have displaced general, social objectives sought through the market.

Union power impoverishes workers and consumers

But even if the unions could no longer dictate to legislators, they could, as the law now stands in most countries, continue to restrain market freedom. As we have seen, such power means denying civil and human rights to some individuals, both as consumers and potential producers. Through strike-threat power, millions are denied the right of access to the bargaining table, and those who suffer most are the initially less able and the 'non-preferred'. Through subterfuges such as apprenticeship requirements, 'the rate for the job', and so forth, strike-threat power has suppressed freedom and impoverished millions. The unions have, indeed, erected what seems to be an almost unscalable wall against the right of all to obtain the valuable general education and technical training which it would be profitable for managements to supply if recruitment were unrestrained. Through society's tolerance of usurpation by the private use of coercive power, freedom of access to the public as consumers (mainly *via* corporate inter-mediaries) has been withheld.

Union power, whether exercised through government or through the strike-threat, far from redistributing income from the rich to the poor, has had exactly the opposite effect. Yet opinion-makers and the public have been conditioned into believing that increased distributive justice has been its aim and achievement. Although at times, through private coercion, some part of investors' property has been seized and squandered, backlash reactions upon the subsequent composition of the stock of assets have soon offset the gains. Any long-run benefits which some unions have won for their members have been at the expense of competing workers who have been laid-off or excluded, and to the detriment of all as consumers. The system has had a formidable depressive effect upon aggregate purchasing power (as distinct from aggregate money-spending power). In other words, union power has reduced the magnitude of the wages-flow and real income and has therefore caused creeping, crawling, chronic inflation to be politically expedient.

The New
Anti-Trust Economics

Basil Yamey

Basil Yamey

B. S. YAMEY was born in 1919 in Cape Town, South Africa, and graduated at the University of Cape Town. After teaching at Rhodes University, Grahamstown, and at the University of Cape Town, he joined the staff of the London School of Economics (University of London) in December 1947, where he has remained except for a year at McGill University, Montreal. Appointed Professor of Economics in January 1960. Member of the Monopolies and Mergers Commission, 1966-78. Elected a Fellow of the British Academy, 1977.

Professor Yamey's publications include *The Economics of Resale Price Maintenance* (1954); (with P. T. Bauer) *The Economics of Under-developed Countries* (1957); (with R. B. Stevens) *The Restrictive Practices Court* (1965); (ed.) *Economics of Industrial Structure* (1973); (jt. ed.) *Economics of Retailing* (1973); (with B. A. Goss) *Economics of Futures Trading* (1976); and articles on the history and economics of distribution; the economics and law of monopoly and restrictive practices; commodity markets and futures exchanges; less developed countries; and the history of accounting.

Professor Yamey is a former member of the Advisory Council of the IEA (1962-84), and since 1985 has been a member of its board of trustees. He wrote its first Hobart Paper, *Resale Price Maintenance and Shopper's Choice*, in 1960 (4th Edition, 1964), and contributed 'Commodity Futures Markets, Hedging and Speculation' to *City Lights* (1979).

66

The New Anti-Trust Economics

BASIL YAMEY

THE revolution—or counter-revolution—in macro-economic theory has been a clamorous and dramatic affair. Within the economics profession it has provoked much dissension, but also a surprising degree of agreement, so that the subject will never be the same again. And its effects on policy have been striking.

A much quieter revolution has been taking place in micro-economic theory, notably in the United States, especially in the part of micro-economics that can be called anti-trust economics. The changes represent, perhaps, more a significant shift in emphasis than a major reconstruction of theory. 'Revolution' may be too strong and colourful a word, but the new analysis has been influential in the United States, where it has led, in particular, to a more relaxed as well as a more carefully articulated attitude in government policy towards mergers and so-called vertical restraints on competition.

One achievement has been to give the *coup de grace* to a policy proposal that was widely supported in the United States in the 1960s and early 1970s. The theoretical and empirical work associated with the quiet revolution has undermined the previous orthodoxy, which saw high concentration as a major cause of non-competitive pricing and monopoly profits. The proposal from this orthodoxy was that industries in which concentration exceeded some benchmark should, in effect, be subjected to compulsory dismantling. This proposal for drastic industrial surgery was supported by several leading academic economists and lawyers (including Professor William Baxter, who was later to become an influential advocate and implementer of the new approach of the 1980s). It began to lose

67

support in the 1970s, and its revival is now quite inconceivable.[1]

The more extreme of the anti-trust revolutionaries have not seen some of their cherished ideas bear fruit. Some, for example, have argued that there is no need for anti-trust authorities to be concerned about supposed monopoly or the market power of monopolies or so-called 'dominant' firms in the private sector. They have contended that if a firm attempts to exploit its market power by restricting output and raising prices, new suppliers would appear on the scene, so that the interests of consumers would be protected without state intervention. An anti-trust issue arises only when state intervention itself seems to prohibit or inhibit the competition from new suppliers—and that is an issue which is, in principle, easily resolvable.

This extreme view has not gained many adherents (although more might be prepared to argue that, given the costs and imperfections of interventions in private monopoly and the risk that remedial measures might inhibit new entry, there is a case for a non-interventionist policy). In any event, there is some inconsistency in supporting the extreme non-interventionist line on private monopolies and at the same time supporting the root-and-branch condemnation of cartels that is now entrenched in the United States. If new entry can be relied upon to discipline any single-firm or dominant-firm monopoly, surely it can be relied upon, *a fortiori*, to render harmless and futile any cartel.

Importance of entry conditions

The new approach to anti-trust nevertheless places more emphasis, and more explicitly, on new entry in judging the conditions necessary to warrant state intervention. Where entry is judged to be relatively easy, there is no call for the authorities to intervene, whether against a merger or a manufacturer's vertical restraint on distributors or suppliers. The merger or restraint will have no anti-competitive effects (since easy

---

[1] On the proposal and its history, Basil S. Yamey, 'Deconcentration as Antitrust Policy: the Rise and Fall of the Concentration Ratio', *Rivista Internazionale di Scienze Economiche e Commerciali*, February 1985, pp. 119-39.

conditions of entry will preserve competition), and will be profitable for those involved only if efficiency is increased. Similarly, where entry appears to be easy, there is no call for intervention in alleged cases of predatory behaviour.

The now-prevailing emphasis on conditions of entry is not new in the literature on the economics of industrial organisation.[2] But it has certainly given a new slant to merger policy in the United States, as reflected in the *Merger Guidelines* issued by the US Department of Justice in 1982 and 1984.[3] The conditions of entry into the particular market and the availability of competition from abroad now seem to be regarded as more significant than the degree of concentration among domestic manufacturers. One cannot find fault with this explicit recognition of evidently relevant forces, nor with a more careful attempt in the *Guidelines* to delineate what constitutes the relevant market for purposes of anti-trust analysis, both economic and legal.[4]

But it is often as difficult to assess in practice how strongly the prevailing barriers serve as a deterrent to entry in a particular market as to determine the boundaries of that market for anti-trust purposes. Two matters complicate the assessment. First, what sort of entrant is being contemplated? Barriers to entry that might be seen as frightening by a small or newly-formed firm could be viewed as rather trifling by a large firm which is seeking to diversify into the market in question, has ready access to the relevant resources and may have a readily transferable reputation and goodwill. Secondly, there is no

---

[2] 'Absolute monopolies are of little importance in modern business as compared with those which are "conditional" or "provisional"; that is, which hold their sway "on condition" that, or "provided" that, they do not put prices much above the levels necessary to cover their outlays with normal profits. If they did, then competition would probably make itself felt; unless stayed by authority, as is the case with patents, copyrights, and some rights of way.' (Alfred Marshall, *Industry and Trade*, Macmillan, London, 1919, pp. 397-8; also the quotations from Arnold Plant's London inaugural lecture in Professor Coase's paper in this volume (pp. 86-87).)

[3] The 1984 guidelines are dated 14 June 1984.

[4] One can be more sceptical of the substitution of the Herfindahl index of concentration for the older and more familiar four-firm concentration ratio, since both statistical measures rank markets or industries more or less identically, and neither is firmly rooted in any acceptable theory of the behaviour of firms.

agreement in the economics and legal professions on precisely what constitutes a barrier to entry. One definition is that a barrier is something that causes a new entrant to be burdened with a cost not borne (or not borne to the same extent) by the incumbent firm(s). High initial advertising and promotion expenditures are often said to constitute the so-called 'product-differentiation' barrier to entry. Yet incumbent firms also presumably may have had to incur such expenditures when they entered that market.

Moreover, if, as the US *Vertical Restraints Guidelines* of 1985 remark, 'entry . . . will be relatively difficult if . . . it normally takes years for a dealer to establish sufficient goodwill to achieve a significant level of sales',[5] should we not have to inquire into the length of time taken by the incumbent firms to build up their sales volumes? The identification of barriers to entry as well as their assessment in a particular case can bristle with difficulties. The new approach to anti-trust economics unfortunately does nothing to clarify these and other difficulties with which anti-trust authorities in the United States and elsewhere have to grapple.

The above quotation from the *Vertical Restraints Guidelines* points to the importance of time in any discussion of conditions of entry. Elsewhere the *Guidelines* observe that 'the relevant question is whether entry is delayed [by the restraint] for a period that is sufficiently long to affect consumer welfare significantly'.[6] This is true enough. But our knowledge of the factors determining the time-lag between restraint and entry, or of the lag between monopoly profits and corrective entry, has not been sufficiently advanced to help us apply the analysis to the facts of any case other than the simplest. The length of these lags must remain very much a matter of judgement and impression. And the phrase 'sufficiently long to affect consumer welfare significantly' does not contribute to the usefulness of the *Guidelines*.

This quotation on 'the relevant question' leads to another aspect of the new approach. What is the criterion according to

---

[5] US Department of Justice, *Vertical Restraints Guidelines*, 23 January 1985, para. 4.21.
[6] *Ibid.*, fn. 22.

which any particular practice or merger is to be judged? The words used above are 'consumer welfare'. Another formulation used in discussions is 'economic efficiency', or some variant of it. The adjective 'pro-competitive' (as opposed to 'anti-competitive') is also much used. The literature also offers the notion that a restraint is acceptable if it increases output. In more formal exercises it is evident that the notion of economic welfare à la Pareto is usually being applied. All this provokes two comments.

The effect on 'welfare'

The first observation concerns choice. A change in market structure or the introduction of a practice can be an improvement in terms of Paretian economic efficiency or welfare; but it may reduce or limit the choice available to consumers. This is true of most vertical restraints, such as limitation of the number of distributors of a product (in the extreme case, one in each geographical area) or the maintenance of resale prices. Such restraints do restrict choice yet *may* increase 'welfare'. The *availability* of choice is something that business customers and final consumers evidently value. But restriction of choice is not an element that enters into the formal welfare calculus. The notions of choice and consumer sovereignty sometimes consort rather uneasily with the analytical notions of economic welfare and its optimisation. Further, it is certainly not obvious that the analytical notion of economic welfare reflects the criterion implicit in anti-trust legislation in the United States—or that it *should* provide the criterion there or anywhere else. Anyway, except in the simplest cases, this criterion is difficult to apply even if we adopt the conventional, more rough-and-ready form which claims that there is an improvement in economic welfare if the gains of gainers exceed the losses of losers from the change or practice under examination (without, that is, the requirement that the losers be compensated).

The second observation involves the idea that if a change or practice 'increases output', it must imply an improvement in economic welfare. The logical connection is clear: monopoly reduces output; output reduction reduces economic welfare; therefore a practice which increases output cannot be monopolistic but must be pro-competitive; economic welfare is therefore increased. Unfortunately, the criterion of output does not enable us to avoid the difficulties caused by using the criterion of welfare improvement itself.

One reason is that an increase in output of the product in question is not necessarily accompanied by an increase in economic welfare. For example, a monopolist may increase his output and profits by practising price discrimination. But an analytical counter-example can be constructed to show that, provided the discrimination is not of Pigou's (in practice unattainable) first or second degree,[7] welfare can be reduced. Thus some consumption that would occur under a régime of a uniform monopoly price will be frustrated under a régime of imperfect price discrimination (Pigou's third degree of discrimination). The associated loss of welfare may exceed the gain in welfare associated with extra-marginal consumption made intra-marginal by price discrimination.[8] Further, if the practice of price discrimination involves expenditure by the monopolist (in order to prevent or control arbitrage between higher- and lower-priced segments of the market), the additional costs may wipe out any welfare gains without wiping out the additional profits to the monopolist.[9]

Vertical restraints

Similarly, an analytical counter-example can shed light on the effects of a vertical restraint. The new approach to antitrust is often held to imply that vertical restraints between

[7] In first degree discrimination, each unit of the product would be sold at a different price, in such a manner that no consumer surplus was left to any buyer. In second degree discrimination the monopolist would set a number of different prices 'in such wise that all units with a demand price greater than x were sold at a price x, all with a demand price less than x and greater than y at a price y, and so on'. (A. C. Pigou, *The Economics of Welfare*, 4th edn., Macmillan, London, 1946, p. 279.) In both these hypothetical situations, the output would be the same as in perfect competition.

[8] Basil S. Yamey, 'Monopolistic Price Discrimination and Economic Welfare', *Journal of Law and Economics*, October 1974, pp. 377-80.

[9] Oliver E. Williamson, *Markets and Hierarchies: Analysis and Anti-trust Implications*, The Free Press, New York, 1975, pp. 11-13.

manufacturers and distributors will increase output and welfare *provided* the restraints are imposed voluntarily (for his own profit) and unilaterally by the manufacturer (not under duress from distributors). The restraints may well raise the prices paid by consumers, the profit to the manufacturer who imposes the restraints coming from an increase in demand (that is, a shift of the demand curve to the right). But the counter-example shows that the welfare effect can be adverse: the reduction of welfare (through the raising of the price) of those consumers who would buy the product in the absence of the restraint may exceed the gain in welfare of those other consumers who buy the product only because the restraint imposed by the manufacturer serves, say, to increase the supply of information to consumers who respond favourably to it.[10] A critic may say that this analytical counter-example is unrealistic or that it can refer only to the rare exception. But this objection is not cogent. What is realistic or probable is a matter of judgement, not of theory; and there may be other analytical counter-examples as well. A successful counter-example forces the argument onto different ground: the espousal of a policy of *general* approval (or condemnation) of a practice must then rest on a judgement of probabilities and not on a theoretical generalisation.

In the new anti-trust economics special emphasis is placed on the so-called 'pro-competitive effects of vertical restraints'—to give the heading of a section of the *Vertical Restraints Guidelines*. These restraints include allotting each distributor a specified territory or category of customers, and exclusive dealing arrangements under which the distributor may not sell competing brands. Much interesting work has been done on the 'efficiency enhancing functions' of such vertical restraints where their introduction and enforcement are not forced upon the manufacturer by distributors but are voluntarily instituted by the manufacturer in his own interests.[11] The general approach is

---

[10]William S. Comanor, 'Vertical Price-Fixing, Vertical Market Restrictions, and the New Antitrust Policy', *Harvard Law Review*, March 1985, pp. 983-1,002; also the article by Rey and Tirole in L. Pellegrini and S. Reddy (eds.), *Marketing Channels: Relationships and Performances*, Lexington Books (forthcoming).

[11]To simplify the discussion, it is limited to restraints between manufacturers and distributors.

that, on their own, restraints that reduce or eliminate competition at the distribution stage must be against the interests of the manufacturer; a manufacturer will therefore not impose such restraints unless he believes the efficiency gains flowing from the restraints exceed the disadvantages flowing from the restriction of competition among his distributors. It is said to follow that, where collusion or effects inhibiting entry are absent, the restraints are justified as increasing output. The nature of the gains in efficiency depends upon the restraint and the surrounding circumstances. They may stem from such factors as the avoidance or minimisation of adverse free-riding that discourages desirable investment and the provision of pre-sales services by the manufacturer or by distributors; achievement of economies of scale in distribution; reduction in transaction costs; better allocation of risk between manufacturer and distributors; and improvement of product quality. Take an example where the manufacturer of some branded goods gives each of his distributors a local or territorial monopoly, so that they do not compete with one another. This territorial protection reduces free-riding by one distributor on another's advertising and sales promotion expenditures; economies of scale in distribution may be achieved; and transaction costs may be reduced.

Effects on long-term efficiency

But recognition of the efficiencies that may flow from vertical restraints does not prove that such restraints are necessarily in the interests of consumers. First, insofar as such a conclusion is based upon the application of the principles of welfare economics, it is untenable as a generalisation. I have drawn attention above not only to the limitations of the welfare criterion but also, more importantly here, to an analytical counter-example. This counter-example assumes, not unrealistically, that consumers are not uniform, for instance, in their demand for pre-sales services, such as demonstrations and advice. Secondly, there is a much more important consideration, although the precise scope for its proper application must be a matter of judgement based on the particularities of each case.

Vertical restraints imposed individually by most manufacturers of a particular class of product may impose some rigidity on the structure of distribution and the methods used. The restraints may make it difficult for new types or forms of distribution to become established and to spread. In the long term, the freezing of distribution channels and methods may adversely affect the interests of manufacturers of the product and also of its consumers. Further, the suppression or retardation of innovation in distribution can affect not only the class of product subject to the vertical restraints but also other classes of product conveniently handled by the same branch of the distributive trade which do not benefit from the efficiencies assumed to flow from the restraints. It is indeed surprising that this consideration seems to have been largely ignored in the new anti-trust literature, since in other respects it places so much weight on externalities.

I have already indicated that it is not easy to determine the types of situations (as regards type of product, for example) in which this general consideration might be held to be material. But the history of resale price maintenance, not only in the United Kingdom, demonstrates how a vertical restraint on competition among distributors can obstruct or delay innovation. Other vertical restraints can have similar effects. Thus even where manufacturers may impose vertical restraints which they believe will enable them currently to distribute their products more efficiently, they may be damaging their long-term interests by burdening themselves with a less efficient apparatus of distribution than would have otherwise developed (although they would not know it). The formulation of government policy should give some weight to the *general* inhibiting effects on innovation that may accompany vertical restraints. This consideration would not require the policy-maker to second-guess the practical businessman but rather to take into account something the businessman would properly ignore. At any rate, the analysis of vertical restraints should not exclude from its purview such possible but unintended consequences. It misses the point to label vertical restraints as necessarily 'pro-competitive'. They may promote inter-manufacturer competition, as each manufacturer seeks competitively to improve the distribution of his brands. At the same time, they reduce inter-distributor competition; and this reduction can have unintended consequences that ultimately reduce efficiency, especially when the restraints are adopted individually but extensively by all or most of the manufacturers supplying a particular category of products. It will be interesting to see how the *Vertical Restraints Guidelines* are interpreted on the requirement that attention be given to the effects of vertical restraints on new entry into distribution.

The example of resale price maintenance

The new developments in anti-trust economics have led to some questioning of the previous almost universal condemnation by economists of resale price maintenance, a type of vertical restraint. The analysis that lies behind the formulation of the *Vertical Restraints Guidelines* of 1985 applies, *mutatis mutandis*, to vertical restraints such as restriction by the manufacturer of the number of distributors, each with territorial protection, as well as to the imposition by a manufacturer of the resale prices below which his distributors may not sell his products. Indeed, the figure of the free-riding, price-cutting retailer destroying brand-goodwill has featured in the economic and legal literature of resale price maintenance for half a century or more. Thus, some American scholars have been advocating that the current stigmatisation of resale price maintenance as illegal *per se* under federal law should be replaced by the more relaxed treatment of the practice as one which should more appropriately be assessed under the rule of reason (subject to the usual caveats about collusion). The *Vertical Restraints Guidelines*, interestingly, do not signal any change in the present position.[12]

The matter cannot be pursued here in any detail. But it seems that the discussion of the new anti-trust economics in the

[12]At this point it is worth noting that resale price maintenance was the subject of the first *Hobart Paper* published by the Institute of Economic Affairs. As the author, I recall the considerable encouragement and help given me by Arthur Seldon who, indeed went on to master-mind and influence a long series of *Hobart Papers*.

United States has largely ignored developments that have taken place elsewhere. Resale price maintenance has been abolished, or virtually so, in several countries, including the United Kingdom, Canada, Sweden and Australia. Yet there is, I believe, no documented and reasonably unambiguous demonstration that any manufacturer of branded goods or consumers in general have suffered from the termination of the practice. The efficiencies often claimed for price maintenance appear to have been non-existent, unimportant or readily achieved by some other means in the trades affected. Again, there is no real pressure by manufacturers (or consumers) that resale price maintenance should be restored where it has been removed. Further, only a few manufacturers in the UK have tried to continue their control over resale prices by establishing (before the Restrictive Practices Court under the 1964 statute) that their use of resale price maintenance benefitted consumers. All this is not, of course, conclusive evidence that vertical minimum price restraints can never promote efficiency. But it does suggest caution when deciding what weight to give to theoretically possible efficiencies.[13]

Still no blueprint

Anti-trust or competition policy poses something of a dilemma for liberal economists. On the one hand, they appreciate the necessity of a legal framework to facilitate and safeguard the operation of markets. On the other hand, they are wary of state interventions in the working of particular markets, however well-intentioned they may be. The dilemma would disappear if, miraculously, it were possible to devise a legal framework which would achieve the desired results without calling

---

[13]A useful set of papers by various authors is published under the heading 'Resale Price Maintenance: Theory and Policy in Turmoil' in *Contemporary Policy Issues*, Spring 1985, pp. 1-58. *Cf.* also G. F. Mathewson and R. A. Winter, 'An Economic Theory of Vertical Restraints', *Rand Journal of Economics*, Spring 1984, pp. 27-38; H. P. Marvel and S. McCafferty, 'Resale Price Maintenance and Quality Certification', *Rand Journal of Economics*, Autumn 1984, pp. 346-359; and the informative study published by the Bureau of Economics, Federal Trade Commission: Thomas R. Overstreet, Jr., *Resale Price Maintenance: Economic Theories and Empirical Evidence*, Washington DC, November 1983.

for the exercise of judgement by government or for any discretionary interventions.

This rapid review should show that the new anti-trust economics cannot provide the blueprint for such a framework of an anti-trust rule of law. Its main architects would not claim that it does. (In American parlance, its principal contributions have been to support the substitution of the sway of the 'rule of reason' for the sway of *per se* illegality in a number of anti-trust problems rather than for the extension of the scope of *per se* prohibitions or authorisations. In this respect, at least, the general tendency of the new anti-trust economics has been in the direction of the pragmatic approach embodied in the British legislation.) Nevertheless, their writings are refreshing and illuminating; and neither anti-trust economics nor the economics of industrial organisation will be the same again. Comanor and Frech may be correct in claiming that 'the emergence of a new position as to the competitive implications of vertical arrangements represents a scientific revolution in the economics of market relationships . . .'.[14] It has certainly brought together a number of novel ideas about the operation of markets that have been developing over recent decades; and it has enlivened and opened up an important branch of study and policy.

---

[14]William S. Comanor and H. E. Frech III, 'The Competitive Effects of Vertical Agreements?', *American Economic Review*, June 1985, p. 545. The sentence quoted in the text runs on: '. . . and we need to be careful not to go too far'.

Professor
Sir Arnold Plant:
His Ideas & Influence

Ronald H. Coase

Ronald H. Coase

RONALD H. COASE is the Clifton R. Musser Professor Emeritus at The Law School, University of Chicago. He was born in 1910 and educated at the London School of Economics. He was Sir Ernest Cassel Travelling Scholar, 1931-2; Assistant Lecturer at the Dundee School of Economics, 1932-34; University of Liverpool 1934-5; Assistant Lecturer, Lecturer, then Reader at the London School of Economics, 1935-51. He was formerly Professor of Economics at the Universities of Buffalo and Virginia. He was chief statistician at the Central Statistical Office, Offices of the War Cabinet, 1941-46, before going to the USA in 1951.

He has held fellowships at the Rockefeller Foundation, Center for Advanced Study in Behavioral Sciences, Hoover Institution, American Academy of Arts and Sciences, American Economic Association, and is a Corresponding Fellow of the British Academy.

He is author of *British Broadcasting: A Study in Monopoly* (1950), and of several seminal articles dealing, *inter alia*, with general economic theory, the economics of 'social cost', industrial organisation and public policy, including 'The Problem of Social Cost' (*Journal of Law and Economics*, 1960) and 'The Lighthouse in Economics' (*Journal of Law and Economics*, 1974). From 1964 to 1982 he was Editor of the *Journal of Law and Economics*.

Professor Sir Arnold Plant:
His Ideas and Influence

RONALD H. COASE

ARTHUR SELDON was a student of Professor Arnold Plant[1] at the London School of Economics (LSE) and upon graduation he became Plant's research assistant. Plant played a major role in shaping Arthur Seldon's views, as he did for others of his students. Arthur Seldon repaid his debt by editing *Selected Economic Essays and Addresses*,[2] in which were reprinted many of Plant's papers. I will describe Plant's approach to economics and will indicate what it was that he passed on to his students. But first I will recount, in greater detail than was possible in the short biographical note included in the 1974 volume, the unusual journey which ultimately brought Plant to a professorship at the LSE and which helped to fashion his interests and his views.

From engineering to economics

Arnold Plant was born in 1898 in Hoxton in East London, the son of a municipal librarian. He was educated at the Strand School and, on leaving, joined a mechanical engineering organisation controlled by Dr Wingfield, a German engineer and inventor, who came to England in 1902 and became naturalised, later changing his name from Wiesengrund. One of the two companies controlled by Wingfield, the Power

---

[1] I am very grateful to Mr Roger Plant for giving me much valuable information about his father's career and views, and for allowing me to consult his father's papers; to Professor Z. Gurzynski for providing me with details of Arnold Plant's activities at the University of Cape Town; and to Professor H. C. Edey for providing information on Arnold Plant's work at the LSE.

[2] Routledge and Kegan Paul, in association with the IEA, London, 1974.

Plant Company, did important work for the Admiralty, and an agitation based on his 'enemy alien origin' led Wingfield to dispose of his interest in that company in 1918 while retaining control (with a partner) of his other company, the Steam Fittings Company. Returning from a period in the Army, Plant, who had obviously displayed considerable business ability since joining Wingfield's organisation, was made Manager of the Steam Fittings Company in 1920 (at which time he was only 21 years of age).

Plant was advised by William (later Lord) Piercy that he ought to learn something about management before doing much more of it. Living in Hoxton as a boy, Piercy had come to know the Plant family. After leaving school Piercy had worked for a timber-broker but, aided by two small scholarships, became in 1910, at the age of 24, a full-time undergraduate at the LSE, specialising in economic history under Dr Lilian Knowles. After graduating in 1913 he was appointed to the staff of the LSE but on the outbreak of the First World War was absorbed into government service and, the war over, began his distinguished career in business. This included his appointment in 1945 as the first Chairman of the Industrial and Commercial Finance Corporation, a position he held until his retirement in 1964.[3]

It is hardly surprising that Piercy's advice led Plant, in 1920, to enroll at the LSE for the B. Sc. (Econ.); even his decision to specialise in modern economic history, which seems strange for someone whose aim was to learn about management, seems almost certainly due to Piercy's influence. But the Commerce Degree had been created after the First World War with the active support of Piercy and other businessmen, and while at the LSE Plant also followed courses for the B.Com. as an external student. He was awarded the B.Com. in 1922 and the B.Sc. (Econ.) with first-class honours in 1923. Plant's demonstration that it was possible to study for these two degrees simultaneously

---

[3] Plant (with John B. Kinross) wrote the obituary of Piercy for the *Journal of the Royal Statistical Society*, Series A (General), Volume 130, Part 2, 1967. He also wrote the obituary of Wingfield, the other man who played a decisive part in his early career, for the *Journal of the Institution of Electrical Engineers*, Volume 77, July–December 1935.

and with distinction led to a change in University regulations which would make it impossible for this feat to be repeated. Plant enjoyed his time at the LSE but he did not adopt either the protectionist views of Lilian Knowles or the socialist views of R. H. Tawney and Harold Laski. The teacher who had most influence on him was Edwin Cannan, the Professor of Political Economy, whose views and commonsense approach to economic analysis and economic policy were to be reflected in Plant's own work.

At this stage Plant seemed destined to return to business management. His career until then had closely paralleled that of Piercy, and had he gone back to business he would undoubtedly have achieved a similar success. But this was not to be. In the University of Cape Town, South Africa, a proposal for a degree in commerce had recently been approved and in 1923 it was decided to create a Professorship in Commerce. When the position was advertised, Theodore (later Sir Theodore) Gregory told Plant that he would be a fool not to apply. Gregory was then a lecturer in economics at the LSE working under Cannan but, like Piercy and Plant, had taken his B.Sc. (Econ.) in economic history under Lilian Knowles. There were 24 applicants for the Chair but it was Plant who was selected, notwithstanding his meagre teaching experience and his youth (he was 25), no doubt because of his experience in management and the high regard for his abilities held at the LSE.

He took up his appointment in 1924 and set about carrying out his duties with great energy. Most of the teaching for the Commerce Degree fell on him and he lectured on an amazingly wide range of subjects, including banking and currency, insurance, factory organisation and administration, business finance, the economics of transport, public administration and marketing, as well as subjects dealing specifically with conditions in South Africa, such as South African Railways. It was not until 1928 that a senior lecturer, W. H. Hutt,[4] was appointed to assist him. During this period he must also have been collecting the material which he used in the chapter on 'Econ-

---

[4] Professor Hutt's essay in this volume appears in pp. 41-63.—ED.

omic Development' he wrote for the volume on South Africa of the *Cambridge History of the British Empire*.[5]

Apartheid as attack on competition

His academic writings while in South Africa were not extensive (hardly surprising, given the demands on his time of his other duties) and were concerned with South African banking and customs tariffs. The only one of his writings in South Africa which he decided to reprint in *Selected Economic Essays and Addresses*[6] was one dealing with the economic relations of the races, a subject which could hardly be ignored by someone seriously interested in the economic problems of South Africa. The article, 'The Economics of the Native Question', was written in 1927 and published in the journal *Voorslag* (May-July issue, 1927). It was a trenchant attack on the policy of the South African government of separation of the races. Plant argued that the policy arose from a desire to stifle competition from the native peoples and was economically injurious to South Africa. It was competition that forced individuals to co-operate in an efficient way. What the South African government ought to be doing was, by providing educational opportunities and in other ways, to bring the natives into Western society. It was wrong to justify its policy by arguing that the natives were uncivilised while withholding the means which would enable them to become part of Western civilisation. A few quotations will give the flavour of this article:

'. . . the refuge which some degenerate white people are prone to seek in the colour of their skin as a basis for privileged treatment is but one particular phase of the universal habit among the lazy or inefficient of seizing hold of an entirely irrelevant characteristic of their competitors and endeavouring to persuade the general public that it constitutes a sufficient ground for legislation differentiating against that particular class as a whole . . . . If the competitor is a Jew, or a married woman, or an Indian, or a native, or an unapprenticed skilled worker, or a professional man who

[5] Cambridge University Press, Cambridge and London, 1936, rev. edn. 1963, Vol. VIII, pp. 788-836.

[6] *Op. cit.*, pp. 3-17.

did not pay his premium as an articled pupil, then the general public is besought to clamour for legislation which will put an end to the competition . . . . While the provision for native education remains as meagre as it is today, the number of natives who will seek social intercourse and full co-operation with civilised, well-educated people is doomed to remain small . . . . our failure to provide for the native population the opportunities for the fullest co-operation of which they individually are capable is *economically* deplorable; and the depressing outlook of many Europeans towards native questions suggests that the *non-economic* reasons for regretting our lack of intercourse with the native peoples are no less potent'.

In 1930 Plant left South Africa and returned to the LSE to fill the newly-created chair of Commerce ('with special reference to Business Administration'). Plant became responsible for the Industry and Trade group in the B.Com. where his teaching in seminars and lectures had a profound influence on his students. He also taught in the new post-graduate Department of Business Administration which had been started in 1930, and in 1935 became its head. From then on running the Department of Business Administration took up much of his time and energies. Closed down during the Second World War, it was restarted when the war ended; but it never seems to have taken root at the LSE and, on Plant's retirement in 1965, it was quietly allowed to die, a decision no doubt made easier by the inauguration of the London Business School in the same year.

The character of Plant's views and his style emerge very clearly in his inaugural lecture in 1931, 'Trends in Business Administration'.[7] This lecture was clearly designed both to indicate what Plant thought important and to mollify those at the LSE who might be hostile to the creation of a professorship devoted to the study of business. Thus, the Webbs are referred to for their writings on business problems 'from the special angle which [they] have made essentially their own' but without saying what that 'special angle' was. The 'pathbreaking' work by specialists in government at the LSE compar-

---

[7] *Economica*, Vol. XII, No. 35, February 1932, pp. 45-62; not reprinted in the 1974 collection.

ing and contrasting public and private administration is noted. Graham Wallis and Harold Laski are praised for teaching that 'the unfettered expression of our individuality [is] the most precious ingredient of liberty', but in such a way as to make advocacy of a free-enterprise system seem a natural development of their views.

Plant's theme in the main section of his lecture is that the businessman does not dominate the economic system. He is 'merely the organising agent of that relentless controller and employer, the community of consumers'. He has to anticipate consumer wants and

> 'the more accurately he interprets the unspoken wish, the more likely he is to remain in favour, the more able he will be to command the capital and the labour which he needs for his production, and for which he has incessantly to bargain against the other businessmen who also serve the ultimate employer'.

To achieve economic progress,

> 'there is one fundamental condition: the preservation . . . of the freedom of the individual to modify his habitual conduct, whether as consumer or producer, whenever he may believe a change to be advantageous to himself'.

Capitalists oppose capitalism

Businessmen, of course, seek to free themselves from their relentless controller, the consumer, by the use of various defensive devices: advertising, rebates to regular customers, season tickets, coupons, the deferred rebate, trade boycotts and so on. Direct attacks on competitors, however, are not likely to be successful. 'Local price-cutting to eliminate rival traders is expensive; new rivals spring up as soon as the attempt is made to recoup the loss by raising prices.' But so long as the state was not 'interventionist in its attitude towards trade practices, so long as it confined itself to the protection of life and limb and to the eradication of misrepresentation and fraud, the public lost little from the transient victories of monopoly, and gained enormously from the strenuous struggle of competition'. This is not what the state has done. Of 'State intervention aimed at the conservation of natural resources—of oil, timber and the like', Plant says:

> 'There can surely be few fields of State activity in which intervention has been more arbitrary in its manifestations and less securely based on economic principle'.

Particularly in the field of public utilities, state intervention has changed from intervention to *prevent* monopoly to intervention to *promote* it:

> 'It is still perhaps an unsettled question of economics whether the attempts both at control and at public operation do not make bad worse; whether indeed the State is not best advised to leave these undertakings to unfettered private management and apply itself rather to the question of encouraging new enterprises and stimulating competition in these fields'.

> 'The continued profitability of all monopolies is conditional on the absence of alternatives and substitutes. Public control either of the prices charged or of the disposal of aggregate profits places the harassed monopolist in a straitjacket when the time comes for a struggle for existence against unhampered competition. It carries with it an almost irresistible claim to protection against free competition, and the State becomes involved on the side of monopoly in schemes to prevent the public from benefiting from the introduction of new inventions and new processes.'

As is apparent from these quotations, Plant did not think of the study of business administration as being primarily concerned with how to run a business. He studied business practices in order to understand why they existed. His field of interest would be described today, I believe, as Industrial Organisation. His analytical system was unsophisticated but powerful. He thought of the consumer as the ultimate employer, with competition as the mechanism through which the consumer exercised his control. Monopoly he considered to be transitional and usually unimportant. The state had a legitimate role in providing law and order and preventing misrepresentation and fraud. But state intervention was commonly designed to help special interests, did not promote competition but monopoly, and imposed economic regulation which often made matters worse. These were some of the ideas that his students carried away from him. They are now more widely held in the economics profession than they were then.

Intellectual property rights: stimulus or deterrent?

A continuing interest of Plant's was the subject of property and the economic function of ownership. He said that his interest was inspired by reading David Hume's treatment of this subject.[8] No doubt it was, but it is difficult not to see in this, as in other aspects of his work, the influence of Edwin Cannan. At any rate, it led Plant to write articles which rank as his major academic achievements in economics. In the early 1930s he wrote two articles, one on patents for inventions and another on copyright in books, both included in the 1974 volume.[9] In them he questioned the need for establishing property rights in patents and copyright. They did not arise out of scarcity but by setting up a monopoly they created scarcity. He pointed out that British authors had been handsomely rewarded by American publishers even though their works were not copyrighted in America. Furthermore, much invention goes on in many trades, even though the resulting improvements are not patentable. He suggested that, even though the existing law were retained, modifications could be made (such as the use of Licences of Right as a normal practice) to improve the situation. But his general stance was one of hostility. Today his discussion seems somewhat incomplete; but it has to be remembered that it was Plant who opened up the subject, and his articles raised questions which still have not been answered satisfactorily.

After World War II he returned to the subject in his Stamp Lecture in 1953, 'The New Commerce in Ideas and Intellectual Property' (also in the 1974 volume[10]). Here Plant examined the problems created for copyright and analogous protection by recent technological changes, such as the recording of sound and broadcasting. It is an interesting lecture but it lacks the fire of his papers of the early 1930s and it adds little to the analysis in them. It seems clear that after World War II Plant did not continue his earlier research on property, and

[8] Plant's references to Hume can be found in *Selected Economic Essays and Addresses* on pp. 30-31, 35-36 and 169.

[9] 'The Economic Theory concerning Patents for Inventions', pp. 35-56; and 'The Economic Aspects of Copyright in Books', pp. 57-186.

[10] *Ibid.*, pp. 87-116.

it is doubtful whether there was a manuscript on the economics of property, at the existence of which Arthur Seldon hints in his Foreword to *Selected Economic Essays and Addresses*.[11]

Plant's ill-health (he suffered from diabetes) was undoubtedly one reason for his reduced scholarly work after the Second World War. His pre-occupation with the Department of Business Administration was another. His work on government committees must also have had the same effect. Plant had served on government committees before the Second World War. He was, for example, appointed in 1938 as one of the original independent members of the Cinematograph Films Council. But after the Second World War, perhaps because his wartime service as an adviser of cabinet ministers gave him a taste for power and influence, Plant was, as Arthur Seldon indicates, almost continuously engaged on government committees. With his energies sapped by ill-health, such activity, combined with his administrative duties at the LSE, was bound to divert him from scholarly work and it is understandable that his research on property was put aside.

But there was perhaps another reason that this happened. Plant was the ex-business manager who went to the University to learn more about management. He saw it as an important function of the University and it was one that was dear to his heart. His inaugural lecture at the University of Cape Town was on 'University Education for Commercial Careers', and at the LSE, as we have seen, he devoted himself to the Department of Business Administration. For many years Plant was also head of the Commerce Degree Bureau of the University of London. It was no doubt a consequence of his concern with the practical application of economics that he had little interest in developing economic theory. But, as we can now see, improvements in theory were required if useful work on property rights was to proceed. The LSE was, at that time, a temple of truth dedicated to the improvement of economic theory but the economists, except to some degree Hayek, were not interested in business practices, and so Plant got no help from them. Perhaps Plant felt that in his articles of the 1930s he had

[11]*Ibid.*, p. vii.

gone as far as he could in the study of property rights. But for many other purposes, the theory he possessed, the theory of competition, was quite serviceable and, armed with it and a realistic view of what a government could and would do, he was able to destroy many widely-held views and to pass on to his students an approach to economic policy which would protect them from much fashionable error and would enable them to devise policies more solidly based.

Arnold Plant was a good teacher who took a deep interest in his students and he exerted himself to further their careers. The work of his students, Arthur Seldon and others, will ensure that his influence neither dies nor fades away.

Roundaboutness, Opportunity and Austrian Economics

Israel Kirzner

Israel Kirzner

ISRAEL M. KIRZNER has been Professor of Economics at New York University since 1968. Educated at the Universities of Cape Town, 1947-48; London, 1950-51; New York University (Ph.D., 1957). Since 1957 he has taught in the Economics Department of New York University: Assistant Professor 1957-61; Associate Professor 1961-68. Author of *The Economic Point of View* (1960); *Market Theory and the Price System* (1963); *An Essay on Capital* (1966); *Competition and Entrepreneurship* (1973); *Perception, Opportunity, and Profit* (1979). For the IEA he wrote 'The Primacy of Entrepreneurial Discovery' in *Prime Mover of Progress* (1980).

Roundaboutness, Opportunity and Austrian Economics

ISRAEL M. KIRZNER

IN recent decades, the term 'Austrian economics' has somehow come to denote two quite distinct segments of economic reasoning. On the one hand, the term has come to refer narrowly to Austrian capital-and-interest theory, particularly as it has developed from its roots in the work of Eugen von Böhm-Bawerk.[1] On the other hand, it has come to refer to the tradition focussing on competitive-entrepreneurial market *processes* (rather than on states of market equilibrium).[2]

These segments of economic reasoning appear on initial examination to be genuinely independent of each other. It is true that to recognise that the production process which involves capital takes place over time is not at all the same thing as recognising the dynamically competitive character of market processes. And, conversely, to understand the way competitive entrepreneurial activity may generate equilibrating (or other) tendencies, through time, is by no means to recognise the implications of the fact that production takes place over time. All this is no doubt partly responsible for a degree of confusion in doctrinal nomenclature. The description 'Austrian economist' is not always an unambiguous label. The purpose of this essay is to argue that in at least one important respect *both* of these apparently independent segments of economic reasoning

---

[1] For example, J. R. Hicks, *Capital and Time: A Neo-Austrian Theory*, Clarendon Press, Oxford, 1973; and Malte Faber, *Introduction to Modern Austrian Capital Theory*, Springer, Heidelberg, 1979.

[2] For example, Gerald P. O'Driscoll and Mario J. Rizzo, *The Economics of Time and Ignorance*, Basil Blackwell, Oxford, 1985, and my *Competition and Entrepreneurship*, University of Chicago Press, Chicago, 1973.

do reflect a common point of departure. Moreover, to see this connection may throw a helpful light on certain aspects of these two segments. I shall first review each of these segments separately.

Capital-and-interest theory: the implications of 'roundaboutness'

Ever since Böhm-Bawerk, Austrian capital-and-interest theory has revolved around the concept of 'roundaboutness'. This insight—that production takes time—focusses attention on intertemporal allocation of resources, on intertemporal rates of exchange, and on the structure over time of the stock of capital in the economy. Because the passage of time permits us to witness the successive initiation of time-consuming processes of production (and their subsequent successive completions), a cross-section of production activities at a given date will reveal a wide array of processes of production arrested at different stages towards completion, embodying stocks of resources invested already for a wide array of lengths of past time. In the market, exchanges are constantly being made that involve the sale of current services of resources (intended to be used to generate future output), the sale of 'half-baked cakes' (intended to be used to generate future 'fully-baked cakes'), and the sale of finished products (intended to obviate the necessity of engaging in time-consuming production effort). Moreover, the sums paid in such market transactions are often themselves the proceeds of intertemporal exchanges, particularly of short- or long-term borrowing transactions. Thus the entire array of spot and intertemporal prices, including the various money and 'own'-rates of interest,[3] is inseparably bound up with the complex arrays of time-consuming processes of production. These prices reflect, therefore, the interplay of economic decision-making at different times by producers, resource-owners and consumers, and thus express awareness of the physical productivities of different kinds and degrees of 'roundaboutness', as well as the time-preferences of the various market participants.

---

[3] ' "Own"-rates of interest' is a technical term that refers, for example, to the number of future apples obtainable for current apples—that is, the commodity is defined in terms of itself, rather than in money values.

It will be helpful to refer to the following model of a simple economy which involves rudimentary time-consuming processes of production. Consider a 'steady-state' economy[4] in which, each year, current employment combines with (free) land to produce, one year later, 1,000 units of wheat. This production process requires that each year 700 units of wheat are used for seed and wages to workers. During each year these 700 units of wheat are 'advanced' by capitalists/producers who are re-paid, or repay themselves, at harvest time. Out of the entire 1,000 units of gross wheat output available at harvest time 700 units constitute repayment of principal, replenishing the 700-unit stock of circulating wheat capital, and the remaining 300 units are surplus, or profit, or interest revenue, enjoyed by the capitalists/producers. And so it goes on year after year.

A non-Austrian perspective might see this economy in a way which overlooks the time-dimension in production, arguing that the annual output is sufficient both to cover the annual 700 wage costs and to yield the annual surplus of 300. In 1986, 1,000 units are produced: of these, 700 units correspond to the quantity used for seed and wages in 1986, 300 are 1986 profits or surplus. And so it goes on year after year.

But from the Austrian perspective this economy is seen as one in which, each year, capitalists/producers and workers engage in multi-period planning and may participate in ex-changes over time. Workers (and owners of seed) sell current labour and seed to producers for 700 units of wheat. (They thus refrain from using their seed and their labour themselves—with available land—to obtain the 1,000 units of wheat available a year from now.) Producers/capitalists draw on their stock of 700 units of wheat to buy the labour and seed currently available, in order to obtain 1,000 units of wheat a year from now. The 300-unit surplus is thus seen as implicit interest earned by producers/capitalists on their one-year investment (of 700 units of circulating wheat capital). Presumably, if current labour had been used in processes of production shorter than one full year (so that wheat output would have been available, say, in six months), annual output would have been

---

[4] That is, an economy in which there is no growth, so that everything continues as before, from one year to the next.

smaller, expressing a smaller surplus (or 'implicit' interest revenue earned by the capitalists). The time-length of the production process being used presumably reflects, then, first, the producers'/capitalists' awareness of alternative physical outputs to be expected from production processes involving different lengths of time, and, second, the structure of their time preferences. Longer or 'lengthier' processes of production might, perhaps, have yielded a somewhat larger output of wheat, but the additional cost in 'waiting' was judged too burdensome; shorter processes would have avoided waiting a full year (for loan repayment and for receipt of interest revenue) but would have provided too small a volume of annual output.

Clearly there is nothing in this Austrian analysis that, on the face of it, invokes insights concerning market processes, imperfect knowledge and entrepreneurial discovery. If we were to assume universal perfect knowledge, of both current and future conditions, the Austrian perspective on the intertemporal decisions and intertemporal market relationships involved in the model would nonetheless still be valid. The 300 units of profit in our model are not at all to be seen as profit in the pure-entrepreneurial-profit sense. Even if all potential gains from intertemporal trade are already fully perceived and firmly grasped, these 300 units of surplus will continue to be received by the capitalists/producers, given the time-preferences assumed in the model and the productivity of roundaboutness. Apparently this segment of Austrian economic analysis neither depends on nor provides support for those other Austrian insights into the competitive-entrepreneurial character of market process.

I shall nonetheless argue below that Austrian capital-and-interest analyses do dovetail significantly and illuminatingly with Austrian insights on the market process. Let us now briefly review these latter ideas.

Austrian market process theory: the aftermath of opportunity

Building particularly on the work of Mises and Hayek (but thereby reviving insights more or less common to Austrians ever since Menger), modern Austrian economics has emphasised the significance of market *processes*. Where contemporary neo-classical or mainstream economists have seen the market, almost exclusively, as a social engine yielding instantaneously achieved states of equilibrium (in the context of alternative given conditions of supply and of demand), modern Austrians see the market as a systematic but *open-ended* process of competitive-entrepreneurial decisions executed on qualities and quantities of output, methods of production, and bids and offers on the prices of inputs and outputs.

A key insight embodied in this modern Austrian perspective concerns the role of the *hitherto unperceived opportunity*. In mainstream economics (and particularly general equilibrium analysis), the notion of an unperceived opportunity is either completely excluded, or is treated in a manner which in reality defines such opportunities out of existence. For Austrians, on the other hand, it is the systematic sequence of discoveries concerning hitherto unperceived opportunities which constitutes the market process. It is the anticipated gain (the pure profit) from such discoveries that provides the entrepreneurial incentive which 'drives' or inspires this market process.

Mainstream economics, especially mainstream microeconomics, assumes, in effect, that all objectively existing opportunities for pure gain are *instantaneously* perceived and grasped. The notion of an unperceived opportunity is thus excluded. Each opportunity is at once extinguished; at all times opportunities for pure gain are therefore absent. *Apparently* unexploited opportunities for gain observed in the market are explained away by reference to the costs of obtaining the relevant information: the gain, it is argued, is more than offset by the costs. In other words, in this mainstream view, the ignorance responsible for ungrasped gain is never *complete* ignorance: that is, it is always the case that agents at least know what knowledge they lack, and where and at what cost such a lack can be made good. From this mainstream perspective, therefore, learning processes are deliberate, and proceed at a deliberate pace governed by the calculated comparison of the costs and benefits of learning. Market processes are never, contends the mainstream, sparked by the spontaneous imagination of alert or daring entrepreneurs; they consist, rather, in perfectly co-ordinated executions of plans that are, at each and every instant, fully optimal in the light of relevant costs and benefits. Clearly then, in this view, there is never a question of equilibrating or non-equilibrating market pro-cesses—*since the market is*, at each and every instant of time, *already in the relevant state of equilibrium.*

Austrian analysis, by contrast, sees the market quite differ-ently. The decisions being made in markets on any given date are likely to express genuine error; that is, on that date the decisions being made happen (from the perspective of the fictitious 'omniscient observer') to be not the best available to the decision-makers *in the light of the information costlessly available to them.* Possibilities for the capture of pure gain arise, indeed, out of the unexploited opportunities overlooked in the course of these error-laden decisions. These gains were not grasped, not because it was not worthwhile (because of the costs of acquiring knowledge) to learn how to obtain them, but because market participants had no inkling they were available (perhaps because of ignorance of how to set about finding out whether such gains exist, or how to grasp them).

The epistemology of gain

Further, in this modern Austrian view, the perennial existence of hitherto unexploited opportunities for pure gain itself offers a powerful incentive, inspiring entrepreneurial discovery of these opportunities, provided that potential entrepreneurial entry is not arbitrarily obstructed. Competitive entry by alert, imaginative entrepreneurs thus constitutes a sequence of steps inspired, at each turn, by the prospect of pure gain. Such a sequence of discoveries may constitute, in turn, any one of several aspects of the market process and may correspond to the 'gale winds of creative destruction' identified by Schumpeter. Here what is discovered are technological possi-bilities that were, it is evident in retrospect, simply 'waiting to be noticed' by daring, imaginative entrepreneurs. But such a sequence of discoveries may also constitute the competitive process whereby the market price of a product is competed down towards its lowest cost of production. Or it may constitute the competitive process whereby the market converges on the specific desired attributes of given classes of products. Here we witness no grand revolutions in technology or organisation but instead a series of competitive moves in which entrepreneurs implement their hunches about how far as yet untried prices or product qualities offer opportunities for pure gain.

These Austrian insights into the character of the market process seem to hold no apparent relevance for issues involving capital-and-interest theory. It is true that the market process is a process of learning through time. But the sense in which time is significant for the market process is, at least analytically, distinct from the sense in which time enters into the Austrian analysis on capital-and-interest questions. Here its importance is that production which uses capital involves intertemporal decision-making. Time enters into the analysis of market processes because such processes unfold through time as sequences of episodes of learning—even where no intertemporal decisions are under consideration at all.[5]

It is, of course, true that real-world entrepreneurs are likely to be capitalists. (A number of writers have roundly criticised the analytical isolation of the pure entrepreneur.[6] My views on this issue have been expressed elsewhere.[7]) But the circumstance that real-world decisions that are related to capital-and-interest theory are likely at the same time to make relevant the theory of the competitive-entrepreneurial market process (and *vice-versa*) does not of itself reveal any common point of departure for these two segments of theory. I nonetheless still hope to show that such a common starting-point can be identified, and that such an identification can throw a useful light on both segments of Austrian thought.

---

[5] Of course, the market process refers also to processes of learning that are related to intertemporal decisions; moreover, the phenomenon of the market process itself generates complicating opportunities for intertemporal speculation. But even if all such intertemporal considerations were to be absent, the essential character of the market process through time would remain.

[6] For example, Murray N. Rothbard, 'Professor Hébert on Entrepreneurship', *Journal of Libertarian Studies*, Vol. VII, No. 2, Fall 1985, pp. 282-284.

[7] *Perception, Opportunity and Profit*, University of Chicago Press, Chicago, 1979, Chapter 6.

Subjectivism and the economics of undervaluation

Both of these segments of theory rely crucially on the notion of *undervaluation* as a driving force in economic decision-making; and the possibility of such a driving force itself depends heavily on the *subjectivism* that has always been central to Austrian analysis. Acceptance of these assertions not only draws the two segments together; it also illuminates our understanding of the real-world decisions that are the subjects of these two separate bodies of analysis.

That the Austrian understanding of the market process reveals its driving force to be undervaluation follows from recognition of the *entrepreneurial* character of that process. Each entrepreneurial step in this process consists of an action inspired by the prospect of pure entrepreneurial profit. But that profit occurs only where the market yields two distinct market values for the same item. Whether one is concerned with pure arbitrage profit (with the speculative profit won by buying low and subsequently selling high), or with profit won by the producer inspired to undertake production of an item that consumers discover to be immensely interesting—profit results from the market permitting the entrepreneur to acquire something at a lower price than that at which the market itself is willing to buy the very same item (or items produced from it). In other words, entrepreneurial profit occurs when an entrepreneur has become alert to the existence of an undervalued item available on the market. Such undervaluation is relative to the 'true' value which the entrepreneur knows (or believes he knows), or thinks he can create. It is the alertness of the entrepreneur to this difference between the market value and the 'true' value of an item, that spurs entrepreneurial re-allocation of the item from lower to higher, more optimal, uses.

The phenomenon of perceived undervaluation can be understood only in terms of subjectivist insights. Undervaluation occurs as a result of failure by market participants to recognise the true (that is, potential) value of an item. Awareness of such undervaluation requires that someone, some alert entrepreneur, interpret the world differently (more accurately) than the rest of the market has interpreted it. Values are not determined by objective conditions but by subjective interpretations and by subjective hunches about them. Economic progress, to the extent that it is driven by entrepreneurial discovery and innovation, is inspired by the differences in valuations generated by such interpretations and hunches.

It may not be equally apparent that Austrian insights on capital-and-interest issues similarly involve perceived undervaluation. Consider what occurs when a capitalist advances resources to allow an entrepreneur to command the services of current inputs in order to achieve output which will be available only in the future. The owners of these current inputs make their input services available at a (low) price which reflects their own (higher) time-preferences. (They apply a high rate of discount in arriving at their present valuations of the future output their services can produce.) The entrepreneurs, on the other hand, recognise that, for capitalists (whose time-preferences are lower), the value of these current input services is much higher. For capitalists, using the lower rate of discount, the present value of the future output is much higher than it is for the owners of current input services. It is the difference between the low value (placed on anticipated output by current input owners) and the high value (placed on that same output by capitalists) that inspires the producers' decision to engage in roundabout methods of production. From the perspective that discounts the future less sharply, the higher value is the 'truer' value of these input services; thus their lower current market price represents an undervaluation. It is the subjectivist perspective, of course, that accounts for such differing valuations of the same future output. To see how it is indeed the perceived 'undervaluation' that drives the capitalistic production process, consider the simple model of the time-consuming production of wheat discussed above. In that model 700 units of wheat were advanced each year to yield 1,000 units one year later.

Now, in a closed and static 'Crusoe' economy (with Crusoe 'advancing' 700 units of wheat to support his efforts this year, resulting in 1,000 units of wheat available a year later) no such undervaluation would be apparent. Crusoe prefers 1,000 future units to 700 present units; that is all. What 'drives' his steady pattern of investment is simply the productivity of roundaboutness. (His time preferences determine the margin at which additional roundaboutness is no longer seen as attractive.) But in a market economy the initiation of roundabout methods of production calls for the purchase of current input services and their commitment to the production of future, rather than for more immediately forthcoming, output. What inspires such commitment is the perception by producers of a difference in the valuations placed on future output by input owners and capitalists, respectively.

To be sure, Austrians are not predisposed to refer to the lower present (high-time-preference) valuations placed on future output as representing 'undervaluation'. From the subjectivist perspective a lower time-preference is no more 'true' than a high time-preference; the high present values that reflect a lower time-preference are no more 'correct' than the lower present values that express a high time-preference. Different persons value given future receipts differently; each valuation is as valid as any other. Nonetheless, when the future arrives and becomes the present, the previously diverse valuations converge until all valuations support those made earlier by the least 'impatient' among the market participants. To be sure, these upwardly-revised valuations (on the part of the more 'impatient' market participants) are not really revisions at all; the new valuations are made at a different time from, and are hence not commensurable with, the earlier valuations. Nevertheless, there surely is a sense in which a market participant treats his present valuation of a presently available good as more 'truthful' than his earlier valuations in anticipation of that availability. In this limited (perhaps metaphorical) sense, we may say that what drives the adoption of more physically productive, roundabout methods of production is the 'undervaluation' of future outputs on the part of owners of current input services (as judged by those whose time-preferences render them less impatient).

Entrepreneurial capital-using decisions

Entrepreneurs assemble resources to produce products. In a capital-using world, the outputs emerge only at some date later than that on which the original resources are assembled. Economic progress occurs when current resources are applied, in appropriately roundabout methods of production, towards the production of output, the value to consumers of which has been generally underestimated. The Austrians see market agitation as being inspired by the drive for gains generated by subjectivistically-based diversity in valuations. Where such agitation places resources in the hands of entrepreneurs who more correctly anticipate future conditions, where it inspires the diversion of resources away from more immediate enjoyments in favour of (what from the perspective of the future will appear as) the more valuable future outputs, this agitation will be seen to have constituted economic progress. The view of the classical economists who somehow failed to distinguish between pure interest and pure entrepreneurial profit (as components of the total share of output received by the classical capitalist class) is seen to have a certain plausibility, precisely from the Austrian perspective. There *is* a significant sense in which the classical profit expresses a single economic entity—and it is Austrian subjectivism (paradoxically so central to subsequent analytical distinctions within that classical profit entity) that throws light on that singleness.

From Macro to Micro via Rational Expectations

Patrick Minford

Patrick Minford

A. P. L. (PATRICK) MINFORD has been Edward Gonner Professor of Applied Economics, University of Liverpool, since 1976. Formerly Visiting Hallsworth Resarch Fellow, University of Manchester, 1974-75. Sometime Consultant to the Ministry of Overseas Development, Ministry of Finance (Malawi), Courtaulds, Treasury, British Embassy (Washington). Editor of *National Institute Economic Review*, 1975-76. Author of *Substitution Effects, Speculation and Exchange Rate Stability* (1978), and *Unemployment—Cause and Cure* (1983), and of essays published in *Inflation in Open Economies* (1976); *The Effects of Exchange Adjustments* (1977); *On How to Cope with Britain's Trade Position* (1977); *Contemporary Economic Analysis* (1978). He contributed papers to two IEA Seminars: 'Macro-economic Controls on Government', in *The Taming of Government*, and 'Monetarism, Inflation and Economic Policy', in *Is Monetarism Enough?*. He also contributed 'Restore Market Momentum and Fight On' to *Could Do Better* (1982).

From Macro to Micro via Rational Expectations

PATRICK MINFORD

I first met Arthur Seldon sometime in the late 1970s. I can't remember exactly when, but I do remember the deep suspicion in which he clearly held me as a 'macro' man. Micro and markets were good, but macro was a denial of markets, a construction around national income accounts which came up with 'GNP', a misleading aggregate in the name of which 'policy levers' were pulled. These levers, needless to say, did considerable damage to the operation of markets; they included a variety of controls (prices, incomes, exchange, credit), changes in government spending (mostly upwards), manipulations of tax rates, and movements in interest rates often against market forces. The conclusion seemed inescapable: all macro must be bad.

The Seldon instinct was right. In succeeding discussions and in my own personal struggle to escape from my intellectual 'macro' heritage, I have come to see the major macro problems as at root resolvable only by micro changes which tackle legal and institutional obstacles to the free play of individual incentives in the market-place.

There are three major macro problems, actual or supposed: inflation; poor trend behaviour of output, employment and unemployment; and the extent of fluctuations around these trends.

Output and unemployment trends

Of the three problems, it should be obvious that poor *trends* in output and unemployment can be due only to micro causes. One of the key results that emerged from my researches into the

107

behaviour of the UK economy was that the steady and accel-
erating rise in UK unemployment could not be explained by
traditional macro-economic analysis. We could identify in the
periods of recession and recovery some speeding up or slowing
down of this progress, but that was all. It followed that a
major research priority was to produce a theory that could
account for UK unemployment.

In retrospect, this task was neither difficult nor original; it
involved taking the insights of classical labour-market analysis
and translating them into the language of macro-economic
or aggregate analysis. Earlier attempts had been made and
were there to be built upon. They had also been rejected con-
temptuously by the Keynesian establishment on a variety of
empirical grounds, mostly valid as it turns out. But in their
joy at rejection, these economists failed to see that their own
theory was failing miserably to account for the facts, and so
they neglected to look to their own backyard. So it was that
the new classicals beat them to it in a theory of unemployment,
and now the Keynesians too (e.g., Professors Layard and Nickell
of LSE and Oxford respectively) are adopting the new classical
analysis, with minor cosmetic variations, to perform this task.
I would now say with confidence that the consensus view of
unemployment is a *micro* view. Unemployment is high because
there are strong incentives to create it. Thus people's unwillingness to take jobs, firms' unwillingness to take on people rather
than machines, unions' power to obstruct, have all been
strengthened by a long series of usually well-meaning government interventions, especially in the name of social welfare and
'compassion'.

The role of rational expectations

Rational expectations—the theory that people use information
efficiently in forming their expectations—played an important
part in this research. It brought out with brutal clarity the
impossibility of accounting for unemployment by the traditional macro-economic analysis, which relied on inertia and
irrationality in expectations. When that element is taken away
from the traditional analysis, the old Keynesian story, that

high and persistent unemployment is due to inadequate demand stimulus by government, is quite untenable. 'Demand stimulus' or 'deflation' could account only for 'cyclical' movements in unemployment, not for its steady progress. True, such cyclical movement could be prolonged and may not be negligible. But rational expectations implied what commonsense in any case would have indicated, that Keynesianism could not explain a cumulative rise of unemployment from 2 per cent in the early 1960s through 5 per cent in the mid-1970s to 13 per cent in the mid-1980s.

It was fashionable to dismiss rational expectations in the early 1980s, not only in this country but even in the USA, and certainly on the Continent and in Japan. It was argued widely that its central prediction—that inflation would come down rapidly and substantially and that output, after a probably sharp setback, would recover and grow—was hopelessly optimistic. Both Mrs Thatcher's and Mr Volcker's counter-inflation policies were dismissed as 'experiments', speculative deviations from the Keynesian orthodoxy.

Some predictions were certainly optimistic; I for one plead guilty to underestimating the 1980-81 recession. But allowing for the occasional and inevitable misjudgements on specific forecasts, the general prediction from rational expectations was correct. Inflation did come down, dramatically more and faster than the Keynesians thought, and about as much as was forecast by rational expectations. In the UK inflation has come down from 20 per cent to around 5 per cent, and in the OECD as a whole from over 10 per cent to under 4 per cent. As for output, it has been recovering steadily since early 1981 in the UK and since the end of 1982 in other OECD countries.

In choosing between 'paradigms', a dramatic test of predictions is often crucial. This recent episode appears to have served as a litmus paper. Many people now accept that rational expectations is not just an elegant and mathematically convenient piece of theorising, but that it is also empirically strong. So it has become widely accepted. All the major traditionalist macro-economic modelling groups, from the London Business School and the Treasury to the National Institute, are now building rational expectations into their models. This major advance spells the death knell of the variants of Keynesian analysis we have come to expect from these groups. Although there *are* ways of preserving Keynesian analysis in spite of rational expectations, they are not appealing to the average economist because they involve theoretical contradictions with the principles of rationality so accepted. Examples are the arguments that wage contracts fixed in money terms will not be re-negotiated in the face of policy changes even though they were written implicitly assuming a particular policy régime, or that markets do not clear even though rational people can see that they are *not* clearing and know what to do about it.

A micro view of business fluctuations and inflation?

'Well,' it may be said, 'I accept your contention that the trend in unemployment and output must be a micro matter. But the business cycle and inflation are surely macro affairs. Having disposed of trends we can surely go back as macro-economists to our traditional modes of analysis but simply apply them to inflation and to the deviations of output and employment from their trends.'

There is a sense in which this assertion is true. It is possible to understand, and to predict in a reasonably useful way, general movements in output, prices and employment. Rational expectations analysis tells us that people going about their business in a sensible manner will interact in certain broad ways. We can usefully identify the forces of aggregate demand and supply. The theory tells us that, if money is created by governments to finance their deficits, prices will rise, and that if it is substantially unexpected, it may temporarily increase output, essentially because people are confused by rising wages and prices into thinking their businesses or households are doing better than they really are. We can then say things about what policies on money and deficits are necessary to avoid inflation and what the effects of policy shocks may be on output. We can also forecast where inflation and output will settle down if policy remains unchanged and we can have a stab at the path they will all take. In the Liverpool *Quarterly*

Economic Bulletin Kent Matthews and I with other colleagues have been trying to do this with particular relevance to the UK since early 1980. We believe this exercise has been quite useful, if only as an antidote to the misguided prognostications and proposals for ambitious intervention by Keynesian analysts.

The necessity of caution

Nevertheless, rational expectations tells us that, because the economy is the interaction of a multitude of rational individuals obeying their own incentives, we have to be extremely careful and modest in this endeavour. Since policies are a sequence and not a single event, their effects depend crucially on how individuals perceive not only the immediate policies but what may follow them. This truth puts the issue of credibility and permanence at the centre of the stage. The effects of a 'given set of policy actions' may be quite different depending on the general sequence of which the actions are seen to be part. For example, growth in the money supply can be regarded as a signal of *further* growth, or as an *aberration* to be reversed as soon as possible, or as a *one-off* increase not to be repeated but also not to be reversed. The effects on prices, output and employment will differ materially, even in direction. Prospective permanently higher growth in money supply will raise interest rates and may, through a financial 'confidence' crisis, even lower output as well as increasing inflation rapidly. A one-off increase may well raise output and have a slower effect on prices. An aberration to be reversed will have little effect on prices or output and will only disturb the financial markets in the very short term.

Furthermore, impelled to look more deeply at the reasons for this behaviour, we see differently both government attempts to stabilise business fluctuations and the reasons for the government's pursuit of inflationary policies.

Back to micro . . .

Active government policy to stabilise business fluctuations can be effective in principle under quite plausible assumptions.

But first there are real difficulties in its design once we recognise the complex interactions between policies, expectations and behaviour. In particular, there is the difficulty of persuading people that the recommended policies will not be abused by cynical politicians chasing the votes of interest groups, since we know that once expenditures are increased they are not easily brought down again later. Second, there is the question of what activist stabilisation policy achieves, even supposing it can be made properly effective. Thus people can work out what is best to do for themselves and business fluctuations, *before* the government intervenes, express those individual choices. One is driven to arguing that 'stabilising' the economy improves matters only if existing choices are inherently biased by some market distortions—which is a pure 'micro' issue.

A good example is unemployment benefits, which cause people to choose more unemployment than is intended by policy-makers. Even if people so choose, stabilising the economy when it is in recession would at least improve its operation. But what a curious way to proceed—using stabilisation policy to moderate the effects of bad micro policy in distorting the labour market through unconditional social benefits. Better surely to remove the intervention or to moderate its effects directly, for example by a proper 'work test' ensuring that only those who are genuinely seeking work receive support.

. . . *and politics*

As for inflation, its technical explanation is monetary. But we must ask what political processes and pressures from interest groups impel the use of monetary policy to create inflation. At once we are immersed in the study of the political market on which Arthur Seldon has written extensively. Politicians themselves respond to incentives. They inevitably seek to please their supporters, without whom they could not survive, and to attract floating voters, without whom their own objectives cannot be achieved. The difficulty in this particular micro study is to know how incentives can best be changed. Exponents of 'public choice' have argued that the democratic process cannot aggregate people's preferences effectively because individual voters have too little incentive to be well-informed while concentrated interest groups have strong incentives to exercise all means of persuasion. Yet this argument flies against rational expectations. A politician is by nature an intermediary who gains power from conveying information and well-matched policies in a package designed to create a coalition of popular interests. For example, everyone would, at least mildly, prefer lower taxes but some dislike strongly the consequential cuts in state spending. So the politician can advocate all the desirable consequences of the tax cut and expose the interested motives of those who oppose it. If he is doing his job effectively, the voters will get all the information they require with no particular effort and could exercise their votes to defeat the vested interests. So this argument against democracy will not do.

Another argument is that the majority may despoliate the minority as, for example, inflation effectively cheats 'rentiers' who hold assets that are denominated in money. The problem with this argument is that it assumes the legitimacy of one set of rights rather than another. Clearly the despoiled would prefer a different allocation of real rewards to the despoilers. But so what? If democracy permits this despoliation, it reflects the distribution of power in the society, and this distribution in turn legitimises whatever the democratic majority does. We have democracy because that is what people will tolerate. It is no good railing against its consequences (unless, as the previous argument had it, they are unintended). The best we can do is to try to understand why they occur. As far as inflation is concerned, it seems reasonably clear that it is in general part of a 'socialist' programme since, at least until it has got out of hand, its consequences have been helpful to the beneficiaries of the programme; in short, it has for the most part been a tax on the better-off who hold money assets.

It follows that inflation is ultimately going to be cured by a *micro* change in the economic *interests* of the floating electorate. Have we not been seeing precisely such a change? Policies to spread home- and share-ownership through council-house sales and privatisation, lower taxes and accompanying lower inflation have helped to change the floating voters' interests.

Surely, too, ideas also have a role in this process; to exercise and enjoy economic freedom requires some assurance that it is right to do so from some 'higher' viewpoint. Yet for years intellectuals have been spreading fashionable feelings of guilt about profit, ownership and 'inequality'. Such anti-market sentiments undoubtedly assisted the onward march of socialism in all parties. Its reversal is increasingly seen in the propagation of the ideas of choice and private effort on which market freedom is based.

Long live counter-revolution!

That is a good note on which to end this essay. For Arthur Seldon has been a tireless champion of these ideas. Macro is micro, but micro needs macro, too, if we are to avoid those 'social cost-benefit' analyses that have unthinkingly and disastrously assumed 'aggregate market failure' (i.e., a Keynesian macro framework). I hope I have now reconciled him to the macro element as he has certainly helped me to understand the micro requirements. Essentially, these ideas form a seamless whole. Are they 'Austrian'? Are they 'Chicago'? They are both and neither. Austrians would be foolish to forgo the benefits of economic modelling, since forecasts and estimates provide clear tests of hypotheses and give ideas a cutting edge in policy debate. The Chicago-style modellers must never forget the shifting sands and springs of individual micro behaviour on which their activities are precariously founded. Let the counter-revolution flourish on all fronts!

The Rise and Fall
of Econometrics

Alan Walters

Alan Walters

ALAN ARTHUR WALTERS has been Professor of Political Economy at the Johns Hopkins University, Baltimore, Maryland, since 1976. He has been a part-time Personal Economic Adviser to the Prime Minister since 1983 (full-time, on secondment, 1981-83). He received a Knighthood in 1983. He was born in 1926 and educated at Alderman Newton's Secondary School, Leicester, and University College, Leicester (now the University of Leicester), graduating B.Sc.(Econ.) (London) with First Class Honours in 1951. From there he went to Nuffield College, Oxford, as a research student and thence to the University of Birmingham as a Lecturer in Econometrics in 1952. He was appointed Professor of Econometrics and Head of the Department of Econometrics and Social Statistics in 1961. Subsequently he was Sir Ernest Cassel Professor of Economics in the University of London (at the LSE), 1968-76.

Professor Walters was an Adviser in Operational Research to the Department of Health and Social Security, 1970-74, and a Member of the Roskill Commission on the Third London Airport, 1967-70. He has held several visiting professorships/fellowships, most recently at Nuffield College, Oxford, (1982-84), and the American Enterprise Institute (1983-).

His principal books (as author, contributor or editor) include: *Growth without Development* (1966); *The Economics of Road User Charges* (1968); *An Introduction to Econometrics* (1968, 2nd edn. 1970); *The Economics of Ocean Freight Rates* (1969); *Noise and Prices* (1974); *Microeconomic Theory* (1977); *Port Pricing and Investment Policy for Developing Countries* (1979); *Britain's Economic Renaissance* (1986).

Professor Walters is a Trustee of the Wincott Foundation and a former Member of the Advisory Council of the IEA, which has published his *Integration in Freight Transport* (1968), *Money in Boom and Slump* (1969, 3rd edn. 1971), 'Land Speculator—Creator or Creature of Inflation?', in *Government and the Land* (1974), 'In Thrall to Creditors?', in *Crisis '75 . . .?* (1975). He delivered the Eighth Wincott Memorial Lecture, *Economists and the British Economy*, in 1978.

The Rise and Fall of Econometrics

ALAN WALTERS

ECONOMETRICS[1] has reached its half-century. It began as a serious subject in the middle of the 1930s, with Jan Tinbergen's famous study for the League of Nations.[2] It promised to turn economics from a speculative philosophy into a scientific discipline. Although only the most optimistic enthusiast expected economics to become a 'hard' science, like physics or chemistry, there was a general presumption that economists might approach the standards of precision and empirical verification in the biological sciences.

Before the mid-1930s, of course, economics had long been regarded as a discipline where the principles were subject to empirical verification. The 19th-century Royal Commissions (e.g., on the Hand-loom Weavers) used economic principles and checked carefully to see whether the evidence was consistent with their ideas. Irving Fisher and Wesley Mitchell[3]

---

[1] My colleague at Johns Hopkins University, Carl Christ, once reported that a new typist in the department, when first hearing of econometrics, typed it as 'economic tricks'. (That was, I think, more than matched by my No. 10 secretary's perspicacity in typing my suitably intoned 'distinguished economic luminaries' as 'distinguished economic lunatics'.)

[2] *Business Cycles in the USA, 1921-1933*, League of Nations, 1939.

[3] Irving Fisher (1867-1947), regarded as America's 'greatest scientific economist' (Schumpeter), was professor of economics at Yale University (1895-1935), and was also a businessman whose directorships included Remington Rand (1926-47). His works include *Mathematical Investigations in the Theory of Value and Prices* (1892, 1961), *The Nature of Capital and Income* (1906, 1927), *The Purchasing Power of Money* (1911, 1920), *Elementary Principles of Economics* (1912), *Stable Money* (1934), *The Making of Index Numbers* (1922, 1927), *The Money Illusion* (1928), *The Theory of Interest* (1930, 1961), *Booms and Depressions* (1932), *Inflation* (1933).

[*Continued on page 118*]

were distinguished pioneers of empirical economics, and both left a lasting impression on such outstanding contemporary economists as Milton Friedman. But neither Fisher nor Mitchell would be regarded as 'econometricians' (or perhaps 'econometrists') in the current sense. The essence of econometrics is the exploration and testing of 'models' derived from economic theory, that explicitly incorporate disturbances, as well as the normal systematic relationships of economic theory. Suppose, for example, we wished to measure the price-elasticity of demand for petrol in the United Kingdom. Our theory of demand suggests that the price is important, together with such variables as the stock and price of vehicles which consume petroleum, even perhaps the price of rail fares. But no theory, however extensive and encyclopaedic, can explain everything. Petrol consumption will vary with the weather, tastes, fashion, and so on. This residual variation, unexplained by the model, is the 'true disturbance', and when we observe these disturbances they are known as 'estimates of disturbances' or, more succinctly, as 'errors'. Thus the econometrician's objective is to explain as much of the systematic variation as possible, and, with luck, describe the remaining disturbances as chance variation with no systematic elements. An analysis of the errors will give us some idea of whether any systematic variation remains in the disturbances.

The statistical problems of econometrics were usually interpreted as the task of pursuing 'efficiency'. Efficiency involves, broadly speaking, designing methods of estimating the parameters (assumptions) of the model, such as the price-elasticity

[Continued from page 117]

Wesley Mitchell was professor of economics at the University of California (1903-13) and Columbia University (1913-19, 1922-44), and director of the New School of Social Research (1919-31). A leading authority on business cycles, Mitchell helped found the National Bureau of Economic Research, regarding his main task as the study of the money economy. Among his publications are *A History of the Greenbacks* (1903), *Gold Prices and Wages Under the Greenback Standard* (1908), *Business Cycles* (1913, 1959), *The Making and Uses of Index Numbers* (1915, 1938), *Business Cycles: The Problem and Its Setting* (1927), *The Backward Art of Spending Money* (1937, 1950), *Measuring Business Cycles* (with A. F. Burns) (1946), *What Happens During Business Cycles* (1951).

of demand for petrol, so that, with the given data, the estimate is likely to be as near as possible to the true underlying value of the parameter. In essence, the econometricians took the classical principle of 'least squares'[4] and much elaborated it so that they could deal with the interacting variables that are so much the stuff of economic models.

In more than two decades, practising econometricians have been much criticised for their concentration on endlessly sharpening these statistical tools of economics. Lawrence Klein, long before being awarded the Nobel Prize for Economics, applied himself to the sharpening wheel. He complained of considerable imbalance between the vast energy devoted to statistical methodology and the little work that was being done in developing data and using the models empirically. As a managing editor of the *Review of Economic Studies* in the late 1960s and early 1970s, I was struck by the paucity of respectable articles in applied econometrics, compared with the ever-rising pile of mathematical theory and methodological contributions.

But despite the protestations of us editors, who protested that we really wanted to publish good *applied* economics, it was obviously in the interests of academic members of the profession to produce economic and econometric *theory*. The effective demand was revealed. With few exceptions, of whom the most notable in Britain was Sir Richard Stone and his co-workers at Cambridge, econometricians stuck to theory and eschewed practice.

It is therefore perhaps not surprising that the major advances in quantitative economics since the Second World War have owed little or nothing to econometric methods (or to mathematical economic theory, for that matter). The first real advance was the development of the 'permanent income hypothesis' by Milton Friedman, or its close relative, the 'life-cycle hypothesis' by Franco Modigliani and Richard Brumberg, which involved no econometrics at all. Indeed, Friedman eschewed the use even

---

[4] Least squares estimation is a method of describing the general relationship between two variables. A line is fitted to numerical values of the variables by minimising the sum of the squares of the distances of the points from the line.

of standard statistical significance tests, and yet the sophisti-
cation and subtlety of his tests of the hypothesis won over most
of the profession. The second considerable advance was the
re-instatement of monetary economics and policy as a central
pillar of macro-economics. Yet again the considerable scholarship which brought about this watershed owed virtually
nothing to econometrics.

Success and failure of macro-econometric models

The ostensible contributions of econometrics to knowledge
appear most obviously in the form of macro-econometric
models. From the pioneering work of Lawrence Klein in the
1950s, following Tinbergen's first attempts, macro-econometric
models encompassing all types of economic régimes as well as
their (trade and financial) interrelationships grew in both
number and size during the 1960s and through the early
1970s. Although the early models had been limited in size and
complexity by the limited capacity of the desk calculator, such
constraints rapidly disappeared with the advent of the com-
puter, and a model of some 700 equations was commonplace by
the end of the 1960s.

   The success of these models in the 1960s in explaining the
behaviour of macro-economic variables, such as GNP, unemployment and inflation, was not striking, but on the other
hand, no opponent could point to any notable persistent
failures. The models were always in a process of development
in attempts to improve their performance in tracking the real
economy. But the modest movements of the Western economies
during that 'never-had-it-so-good' decade showed the models
in their best light. When critics pointed out that such complex
models did not out-perform the more modest methods of extra-
polation, it was claimed that the macro-econometric models
provided insights into the economic process that could not be
obtained by other means. Some modest measure of the success
of the models was the fact that many were privately funded and
prospered by selling their forecasts on the open market. The
acid test of such models occurred in the 1970s with the outbreak
of record inflation followed by the worst recession since the

1930s. They failed.[5] Simple (pejoratively, 'simple-minded') monetarist predictions fared much better.

The failure of the models, precisely when they were most urgently required to succeed, was quite spectacular and it was followed by a number of other 'wrong calls'. This series of blunders contributed, in Britain at least, to the nadir of popular respect for the prediction of economists generally, and modellers in particular. We have only to compare the confident prognostications of disaster which followed the 1981 Budget with the robust recovery that nonetheless ensued.

The reasons for the rather poor performance of macroeconometric models are not clearly understood. Perhaps the most popular view is that, while it is possible to model 'small' changes in government policy, there is no way in which economists—or anyone else—can model a substantial shift. This would require changing the structure of the model if it is to remain at all accurate. The analysis of historical data will provide a treacherous guide to the future, as the economic players adjust to the new régime. For example, up to the end of the 1970s it was widely, and correctly, assumed that if there was any substantial increase in unemployment, government would introduce expansionary monetary and fiscal policies. People could take this Pavlovian government behaviour into account in making their own decisions. But with the advent of the Thatcher Government, policy was changed. This shift had a profound effect on private decisions, but it was impossible to adduce such an effect from the history of the postwar years, which is the raw material of the models.

Econometric models: lurking absurdities

Another major problem arises from the difficulty of understanding the content of such models. I would conjecture that in such large models the investigator ceases to be in control. The complexities of the equations, and their combination, may

[5] I reviewed these failures for the models of the British economy in 'Macroeconomic Models and Policy in Britain', in Michael D. Intriligator (ed.), *Frontiers of Quantitative Economics, Vol. IIIB*, North Holland, Amsterdam, 1977 (papers invited for presentation at the Econometric Society Third World Congress), pp. 809-825.

hide all sorts of absurdities which, under some configuration of circumstances, may appear to haunt the predictions. Experience suggests that it is difficult for modellers to identify absurdities. For example, I have recently reviewed[6] the predictions of (mostly United States) models of the consequences of an increase in government spending, holding tax rates and monetary growth constant, on real GNP (or GDP). All of them predict that, in the relevant period when their results of the models are thought to be trustworthy (certainly up to two years and perhaps up to four), an increase in government spending increases real GNP. But, so far as I can discover, the models *never* predicted a decline in GNP, even under the fullest of full-employment conditions. Oddly enough, this absurdity did not strike many of the modellers, as well as many economists innocent of macro-econometric modelling, as being an unlikely characteristic of reality! I suspect that there are many similar curious effects embedded in the models and as yet undiscovered.

The new Fishermen

It was, in part, the disenchantment with macro-econometric models, based on an increasingly dubious macro-economic theory, that gave rise to the development of a form of atheoretical macro-econometrics.[7] Instead of taking the structure of the model from the postulates of economic theory and placing prior restrictions on the outcome, atheoretical macro-econometrics (hereinafter AM) accepts virtually no such prior specifications. It explores the data free from such preconceptions to examine whether there is 'causality' and 'exogeneity' among variables as demonstrated by the performance of the time-series. Technically these search procedures are called 'vector autoregressions' or VARs, where virtually everything is regressed on everything else—or almost everything. There *is* an admission of economic theory in the sense that the list of variables is not unlimited and, indeed, depends on the pre-

---

[6] *Britain's Economic Renaissance*, Oxford University Press, Oxford and London, 1986.

[7] Probably the best account is to be found in Christopher Sims, 'Macroeconomics and Reality', *Econometrica*, Vol. 48, 1980, pp. 1-47.

conceptions of theory. So far as I know, for example, no VAR has explored the issue of causality in the birth rate and the population of storks. There is a limit—but, as in all such decisions, there is no rule or principle for determining it. In principle anything goes; in practice the limits are conventional. In place of the Popperian principle of concentrating on a simple, precise hypothesis, VARs explore a manifold of hypotheses.

Controversy still rages about the use and abuse of AM and VARs. These methods appear to be the modern equivalent of 'let the data speak for themselves'—a view much savaged by many distinguished economists, Alfred Marshall and Milton Friedman among them. But modern computing methods enable practitioners to examine very large quantities of data and to tease out the most intimate and complex structures, which was quite beyond the powers of economists some two or three decades ago. Instead of testing hypotheses, econometricians can use VARs to seek them—again, a practice roundly condemned as 'fishing expeditions' by the traditional view of scientific inquiry.[8] Yet the VARs have proven to be useful, and probably superior to alternatives, as devices for forecasting and categorising causality. As a statistical matter, this usefulness is hardly surprising since, on the one hand, they use more information than the standard macro-econometric methods of forecasting, and, on the other, they explicitly seek a causal chain in the time-series. The real bone of contention is whether VARs can be used to determine the effects of changes in policy—and it will be a very long time before the jury returns a verdict.

The developments in computing that made VARs such an easy step also had the effect of generating much more applied economics, expressed in more manageable micro-economic terms, as well as stimulating many more excursions into relatively simple macro-models. In my view, there has been a considerable improvement in our knowledge in many appli-

---

[8] In 'Karl Popper and the Jazz Age', *Encounter*, June 1985, pp. 65-74, Dr D. C. Stove has argued that such scientific anarchy is the ultimate development of Sir Karl Popper's basic revolution of the philosophy of science. I have not seen an interpretation of AM and VARS in the light of this idea, but I am sure it would be illuminating.

cations, particularly in the analysis of demand. But this very availability of computing capacity has its dangers. One of my colleagues once observed that econometrics had degenerated to the state where, given enough time, any competent econometrician could always manipulate the data to 'prove' any case you wished. Econometricians had become data masseurs. Instead of seeking data and methods of analysis to disprove a theory, as required by the methodology of Karl Popper and Milton Friedman, the temptation—and, alas, the practice—was to seek a result consistent with the hypothesis.

Individuality upsets 'robustness'

In recent years a few econometricians, worried by this phenomenon, have developed concepts of the 'robustness' of results. Broadly speaking, this 'robustness' requires that the results of an empirical inquiry still stand when the specification of the model is changed in a number of clearly 'acceptable' ways. Again, the general idea is both understandable and laudable, but when translated into practical inquiry many difficulties emerge. I suspect that, since personal predilection and choice still play such a large role in the concept of 'robustness', the latter is unlikely to become the touchstone of applied econometrics.[9]

Finally, it is a shame that econometricians have not really reached that vast audience of informed people who feel inferior when confronted with algebra and are unaccustomed to thinking in stochastic (probabilistic) terms. Much of econometrics remains remote and unaccessible, shrouded in mathematics. This is a pity. Criticism from able colleagues, from economists like Arthur Seldon, who are directly concerned with markets and men and policy and prices in the real world, would substantially improve the subject and increase its relevance. To make econometrics comprehensible is a daunting job—but not, I fancy, one beyond Arthur's prodigious ability, if only he were prepared to spend the bulk of his next 70 years, pen in hand, at the task.

[9] For example, M. McAleer, A. R. Pagan and P. A. Volcker, 'What will take the con out of econometrics?', *American Economic Review*, Vol. 75, No. 3, 1985, pp. 293-307.

Has Liberalism Failed?

Milton Friedman

Milton Friedman

MILTON FRIEDMAN was born in 1912 in New York City and graduated from Rutgers before taking MA at Chicago and PhD at Columbia. From 1935-37 he worked for the US National Resources Committee, from 1937-40 for the National Bureau of Economic Research, and from 1941-43 for the US Treasury. From 1946 to 1977 he taught at the University of Chicago, where in 1962 he became the Paul Snowden Russell Distinguished Service Professor of Economics.

Milton Friedman is now a Senior Research Fellow at the Hoover Institution of Stanford University. He has taught at universities throughout the world, from Cambridge to Tokyo. Since 1946 he has also been on the research staff of the National Bureau of Economic Research. Professor Friedman was awarded the 1976 Nobel Prize in Economic Sciences.

Among his best known books are *Essays in Positive Economics* (1953), *Studies in the Quantity Theory of Money* (ed., 1956), *A Theory of the Consumption Function* (1957), *Capitalism and Freedom* (1962), (with Anna J. Schwartz) *A Monetary History of the United States, 1867-1960* (1963), *The Optimum Quantity of Money* (1969), and (with Rose Friedman) *Free to Choose* (1980) and *The Tyranny of the Status Quo* (1984). The IEA has published his Wincott Memorial Lecture, *The Counter-Revolution in Monetary Theory* (1970), *Monetary Correction* (1974), *Unemployment versus Inflation?: An Evaluation of the Phillips Curve* (1975), *From Galbraith to Economic Freedom* (1977), and *Inflation and Unemployment: The New Dimension of Politics* (The 1976 Alfred Nobel Memorial Lecture, 1977); and his contributions to *Inflation: Causes, Consequences, Cures* (1974).

Has Liberalism Failed?

MILTON FRIEDMAN

IN *Capitalism and Freedom*, which I wrote in 1962 with the assistance of my wife Rose, we labelled the political and economic viewpoint we share with Arthur Seldon and countless others 'liberalism in its original sense—as the doctrines pertaining to a free man'.[1] How have those doctrines fared in the two decades and more since the book was published?

That question breaks down into two others. How have those doctrines fared, first, in the world of ideas and, second, in the world of practice? And what are the prospects for the future?

Intellectual success

The doctrines have clearly fared very well indeed in the world of ideas, as I pointed out in a new preface for a recent paperback re-issue of the book:[2]

'The lectures that my wife helped shape into this book were delivered a quarter of a century ago. It is hard even for persons who were then active, let alone for the more than half of the current population who were then less than ten years old or had not yet been born, to re-construct the intellectual climate of the time. Those of us who were deeply concerned about the danger to freedom and prosperity from the growth of government, from the triumph of welfare-state and Keynesian ideas, were a small beleaguered minority regarded as eccentrics by the great majority of our fellow intellectuals.

Even seven years later, when this book was first published, its views were so far out of the mainstream that it was not reviewed

[1] Milton and Rose Friedman, *Capitalism and Freedom*, University of Chicago Press, Chicago, 1962 (re-issued 1982), p. 6.

[2] *Ibid.*, pp. vi-viii.

by any major national publication—not by the *New York Times* or the *Herald Tribune* . . . or the *Chicago Tribune*, or by *Time* or *Newsweek* or even the *Saturday Review*—though it was reviewed by the London *Economist* and by the major professional journals. And this for a book directed at the general public, written by a professor at a major US university, and destined to sell more than 400,000 copies in the next eighteen years. It is inconceivable that such a publication by an economist of comparable professional standing but favourable to the welfare state or socialism or communism would have received a similar silent treatment.

How much the intellectual climate has changed in the past quarter-century is attested to by the very different reception that greeted my wife's and my book *Free to Choose*,[3] a direct lineal descendant of *Capitalism and Freedom* presenting the same basic philosophy and published in 1980. That book was reviewed by every major publication, frequently in a featured, lengthy review. It was not only partly re-printed in *Book Digest*, but also featured on the cover. *Free to Choose* sold some 400,000 hardcover copies in the US in its first year, has been translated into twelve foreign languages, and was issued in early 1981 as a mass-market paperback.

The difference in reception of the two books cannot, we believe, be explained by a difference in quality. Indeed, the earlier book is the more philosophical and abstract, and hence more fundamental. *Free to Choose*, as we said in its Preface, has "more nuts and bolts, less theoretical framework". It complements, rather than replaces, *Capitalism and Freedom*. On a superficial level, the difference in reception can be attributed to the power of television. *Free to Choose* was based on and designed to accompany our PBS [Public Broadcasting System] series of the same name, and there can be little doubt that the success of the TV series gave prominence to the book.

That explanation is superficial because the existence and success of the TV programme itself is testimony to the change in the intellectual climate. We were never approached in the 1960s to do a TV series like *Free to Choose*. There would have been few if any sponsors for such a programme. If, by any chance, such a programme had been produced, there would have been no significant audience receptive to its views. No, the different reception of the later book and the success of the TV series are common consequences of the change in the climate of opinion. The ideas in our

---

[3] Secker and Warburg, London/Harcourt Brace Jovanovich, New York, 1980.

two books are still far from being in the intellectual mainstream, but they are now, at least, respectable in the intellectual community and very likely almost conventional among the broader public.

The change in the climate of opinion was not produced by this book or the many others, such as Hayek's *Road to Serfdom* and *Constitution of Liberty*, in the same philosophical tradition. For evidence of that, it is enough to point to the call for contributions to the symposium *Capitalism, Socialism and Democracy* issued by the editors of *Commentary* in 1978, which went in part: "The idea that there may be an inescapable connection between capitalism and democracy has recently begun to seem plausible to a number of intellectuals who once would have regarded such a view not only as wrong but even as politically dangerous". My contribution consisted of an extensive quotation from *Capitalism and Freedom*, a briefer one from Adam Smith, and a closing invitation: "Welcome aboard". Even in 1978, of the 25 contributors to the symposium other than myself, only 9 expressed views that could be classified as sympathetic to the central message of *Capitalism and Freedom*.

The change in the climate of opinion was produced by experience, not by theory or philosophy. Russia and China, once the great hopes of the intellectual classes, had clearly gone sour. Great Britain, whose Fabian socialism exercised a dominant influence on American intellectuals, was in deep trouble. Closer to home, the intellectuals, always devotees of big government and by wide majorities supporters of the national Democratic party, had been disillusioned by the Vietnam War, particularly the role played by Presidents Kennedy and Johnson. Many of the great reform programmes—such guidons of the past as welfare, public housing, support of trade unions, integration of schools, federal aid to education, affirmative action—were turning to ashes. As with the rest of the population, their pocketbooks were being hit with inflation and high taxes. These phenomena, not the persuasiveness of the ideas expressed in books dealing with principles, explain the transition from the overwhelming defeat of Barry Goldwater in 1964 to the overwhelming victory of Ronald Reagan in 1980—two men with essentially the same programme and the same message.'

A. V. Dicey put the same point many years ago:

'Success . . . in converting mankind to a new faith, whether religious, or economical, or political, depends but slightly on the strength of the reasoning by which the faith can be defended, or even on the enthusiasm of its adherents. A change of belief arises, in the main, from the occurrence of circumstances which incline the majority of the world to hear with favour theories which, at one time, men of common sense derided as absurdities or distrusted as paradoxes.'[4]

Such basic changes in the climate of opinion have three characteristics. First, as Dicey emphasised, they develop gradually and maintain their dominance for long periods. The belief in mercantilism lasted for centuries, and started to break down only after the middle of the 18th century. The liberal belief that followed began to gain momentum only with Adam Smith's *Wealth of Nations*, published in 1776, and started to break down only about a century later, when socialist ideas gained momentum. Those notions in turn lasted for close to a century.

Second, the changes in the climate of opinion tend to be worldwide in scope. The dominance of the liberal idea shaped both the development of Meiji Japan after 1867 and the stirrings of liberalism in Russia towards the end of the last century, no less than the repeal of the Corn Laws in Britain and the economic policies of the United States in the 19th century. Similarly, the rise of socialist ideas contributed to the triumph of communism in Russia and China no less than to the emergence of the welfare state in Britain and the New Deal in the United States. And the decline of belief in socialism is reflected in the emergence of Solidarity in Poland and market reforms in China no less than in the election of Margaret Thatcher in Britain and Ronald Reagan in the United States.

Third, changes in the climate of opinion tend to affect policy after a long delay. To quote Dicey again:[5]

'The opinion which changes the law is in one sense the opinion of the time when the law is actually altered; in another sense it has often been in England the opinion prevalent some twenty or thirty years before that time; it has been as often as not in reality the opinion not of today but of yesterday'.

---

[4] *Lectures on the Relation between Law and Public Opinion in England during the Nineteenth Century*, Macmillan, London, 1905 (2nd edn. 1914), p. 23.

[5] *Ibid.*, p. 33.

Compare with that Keynes's classic comment on the role of the 'defunct economist' and 'academic scribbler'.[6]

Practical failure

Since, as Dicey stresses, policy lags behind opinion, it should occasion no surprise that the developments since 1962 in the world of practice differ markedly from those in the world of ideas. The United States, for which I know the situation best and with which *Capitalism and Freedom* dealt, is clearly further from a truly liberal society in 1986 than it was in 1962.

A simple measure is the ratio of government spending to national income. For all tiers of government—federal, state and local—spending was 43·8 per cent of national income in 1985, compared with 34·7 per cent in 1962. As a further benchmark, the corresponding fraction was 15 per cent in 1930.

This measure in some respects overstates and in others understates the extent of government intervention. It overstates the extent because government spending includes 'transfer payments'—social security and other government expenditures that are not payments for goods or services—while national income does not. For example, the salaries of the government employees who administer the direct relief programmes in the United States are included in both government spending and national income; the payments to the recipients of relief are included in government spending but not national income. That is why it is technically possible for the ratio of government spending to national income to exceed 100 per cent, as I believe it has done on occasion in Israel.

If the US government were to reclassify the recipients of AFDC—'Aid to Families with Dependent Children'—as government employees assigned to child care, government spending would be unchanged but national income would be increased, thus reducing the ratio of spending to income; and similarly for other transfers. The ratio of government spending to national-income-plus-transfer-payments, which corrects for this source of overstatement, was 14·8 per cent in 1930, 32·4

---

[6] J. M. Keynes, *The General Theory of Employment, Interest, and Money*, Macmillan, London, 1936, p. 383.

per cent in 1962, and 38·5 per cent in 1985. These figures are somewhat lower than the percentages cited above, but the direction of change is clearly the same. In the 32 years from 1930 to 1962, the US government took over from its citizens the spending of 21 per cent of the amount initially under their control; in the next 23, it took over 9 per cent of the remainder. That is hardly a story of the easing of government control.

The adjusted measure, in its turn, *under*states the role of government because many government interventions involve little or no spending of the kind that is entered directly in government accounts; and such interventions have multiplied over recent decades. For example, tariffs and other restraints on international trade involve little government spending—other than for their enforcement—yet may impose large costs on the public, which in principle should be included in government spending. A particularly clear case is the so-called 'voluntary' quotas on imports of Japanese cars introduced by the Reagan Administration in 1981. These restrictions have cost car buyers many billions of dollars, and yet they involved negligible government spending. That assertion is equally true for such interventionist measures as price and wage controls, minimum wages, the host of regulations imposed on business enterprises, the licensure of occupations—and so on in almost endless variety.

An indication of what has happened in such interventionist measures can be gained from a list, which we described as 'far from comprehensive', that we gave in *Capitalism and Freedom*,[7] of 14 'activities currently undertaken by government in the US that cannot . . . validly be justified in terms of the principles' of a liberal society. Of these, only one has been terminated: 'Conscription to man the military services in peacetime'—and that victory is by no means final.

Some improvement has occurred in two others: 'Legal minimum wage rates or legal maximum prices', such as the maximum interest rates that could be paid on various categories of bank deposits. Minimum wage rates are still with us but maximum interest rates on deposits are on the way out. The

---

[7] *Op. cit.*, pp. 35-36.

second improvement has been in the detailed regulation of industries. Airlines have been deregulated almost entirely. Road freight transport ('trucking', in US usage) has been largely deregulated. There has been some, very limited, progress elsewhere—and some backsliding.

Little change has occurred in seven other activities. With tariffs on imports or restrictions on exports, new devices, such as the so-called 'voluntary' import or export quotas, have proliferated, but the growth of foreign trade as a fraction of income makes it difficult to judge whether on balance protectionism has increased or decreased.

Second, in government control of output, there has perhaps been some increase in control in agriculture and some decrease elsewhere.

Third, in the control of radio and television by the Federal Communications Commission there has, again, been some very limited deregulation, but no relaxation at all of the statutory requirement for a government permit to be allowed to broadcast.

Fourth, there has been little, if any, relaxation in the requirements of a licence to practise a broad range of trades and professions, ranging from barbering to medicine.

Fifth, national parks, which we had suggested should be privatised, remain in government hands.

Sixth, the legal prohibition on the carrying of mail for profit endures. The market has been allowed to introduce some competition here, in the form of expensive express mail services, but there has been no move to open up regular first-class mail to competition.

Lastly, publicly owned and operated toll roads which, like national parks, we had suggested should be privatised, are no closer to joining the private sector.

For the remaining four items on our original list of 14, the situation has definitely become worse than it was in 1962.

The first of these is 'parity price support programmes for agriculture': both expenditures and government-stored surpluses have soared.

Second, 'rent-control . . . or more general price- and wage-controls' already worried us in 1962. But then only New York had rent control. In 1986 many more communities do, including such large ones as Los Angeles and San Francisco, and such extreme idiosyncratic ones as Santa Monica and Berkeley, both in California and both under local governance by the extreme left. Moreover, President Nixon imposed general wage- and price-controls from 1971 to 1974. Some of these impositions lasted much longer—the control on oil prices endured until 1981, and that on natural gas is still with us.

Third, to the social security expenditures, especially old age and retirement, of 1962 Medicare has been added, coverage for disability has been massively expanded, Medicaid (medical assistance to the indigent) introduced; and a number of other programmes added.

Fourth, the host of so-called 'public housing' and other subsidies directed in 1962 at fostering residential construction has become even more numerous.

Finally, numerous additions have been made to our even then 'far from comprehensive' list of 14. President Lyndon Johnson launched numerous 'Great Society' programmes in the course of his unsuccessful 'War on Poverty'.[8] In addition, railroad passenger traffic was nationalised under Amtrak and railroad freight traffic partially nationalised under Conrail; Federal government involvement in higher education was expanded; the National Foundation for the Arts and Humanities and two new government departments, Energy and Education, were established. And this list of additions, too, is far from comprehensive.

The practical progress of economic liberalism since 1962 reminds me of a line in a musical comedy of the 1930s, *Pins and Needles*, staged by the International Ladies Garment Workers' Union. If my memory serves me right, it went: 'One step forward, two steps backward. That is the way we advance'.

On a more optimistic note, contrasting the later 1980s with 1962 paints an unduly dismal picture. Although the role of government continued to grow throughout the period, there are significant differences between the earlier and later years. In the five years from 1980 to 1985, no major *new* spending

---

[8] *Cf.* Charles Murray, *Losing Ground*, Basic Books, New York, 1983.

policy was enacted by the Federal government. Federal government spending did continue to increase as a fraction of national income, thanks partly to increased spending on defence but mostly to government policies that had been instituted earlier. In addition, there was some reduction of Federal spending on other programmes, particularly on grants to the States and localities. And a number of individual States adopted constitutional amendments *limiting* state spending. Thus early signs of deceleration—perhaps even of a change of direction—are visible.

What liberalisation in the West?

My knowledge of the developments in other countries is much less detailed than for the United States. Yet the general outline is clearly not very different. In Britain the welfare state and socialism started earlier and went much further than in the United States. Nonetheless, the role of government continued to expand in the 1960s and 1970s. The turn-around started slightly earlier in Britain but, with a couple of exceptions, has, as in the United States, consisted of little more than a mere deceleration rather than a *reversal* of the growth of government. The major exceptions are the elimination of exchange control and privatisation of some government-owned enterprises. However, these exceptions are for interventions that did not exist in the United States.

West Germany is an even more extreme case. Reforms after World War II gave it a reputation, only partly deserved, as a bastion of free enterprise. Throughout the past two decades, however, it has moved away from the free market, a trend reflected in both government spending and government control of the economy. As yet, to my knowledge, there are few signs of any significant reversal of direction.

Interestingly, the most encouraging signs of a recent reversal of direction are in countries that went furthest in a collectivist and welfare-state direction, and they have taken place under ostensibly socialist leaderships: France and Spain under socialist governments; Australia and, even more dramatically, New Zealand under labour governments; and, most remarkably of all, China under a Communist government. I hasten to add that I do not regard the developments in China as presaging the emergence of a liberal society in either economic or political activities. But all these examples are a striking demonstration that ideas do not respect national boundaries.

Prospects for the Future

Intellectual decline?

In 1962 *Capitalism and Freedom*[9] concluded with this hopeful note:

> '[W]e shall be able to preserve and extend freedom ... only if we awake to the threat that we face, only if we persuade our fellow men that free institutions offer a surer, if perhaps at times a slower, route to the ends they seek than the coercive power of the state. The glimmerings of change that are already apparent in the intellectual climate are a hopeful augury'.

That augury has been fulfilled in intellectual circles even more than we could have dared to hope. In 1962 the Institute of Economic Affairs stood almost alone in its courageous, principled, and ultimately effective defence of the market and a free society. Since then the number of such institutes has multiplied, and they are now flourishing around the globe, promoting the same message, although not always as effectively. The so-called left is bankrupt and disillusioned. The remaining true believers in Marx, Lenin, Edward Bellamy, George Bernard Shaw and the Webbs are clearly on the defensive. In many cases, they rely on support, financial and otherwise, open or concealed, from the Communist powers.

But the success of liberal ideas is a mixed blessing. I have long argued that discrimination against liberal intellectuals in academe and elsewhere has been an advantage as well as a disadvantage. The result was that the intellectual and moral quality of liberals who managed to overcome discrimination was higher than of their opponents. Precisely because they were a tiny, beleaguered minority, the liberals came to know the arguments of their opponents better than their opponents

[9] *Op. cit.*, p. 202.

did, and had thought more deeply about their own and their adversaries' weaknesses. Their opponents, even if equal or superior in sheer intellectual quality, had been spared this goad, and as a consequence they were at a disadvantage. And in intellectual wars quality is far more important than quantity.

As the situation has changed, a dilution of quality has, to my mind, accompanied an astonishing increase in quantity. Advocates of the free society of outstanding quality are undoubtedly more numerous than they were two decades ago. But as the total number of advocates has increased even more rapidly, so the *average* quality has declined. Moreover, the less hostile intellectual environment has encouraged an element of complacency and superficiality. Liberals are no longer forced to contend with the unrelieved dominance of opposing views and hence are no longer forced to understand them as thoroughly as we once were, nor to probe as deeply into our own. And yet, unless we understand our opponents' views *better* than they do, we cannot be sure that we are right and they are wrong.

In Dicey's terms, the counter-current is becoming the current, and, as it does, new counter-currents are emerging. Such a process, no doubt, has played a large role in the somewhat cyclical swings in the intellectual climate of opinion I outlined earlier: from mercantilism to liberalism to socialism to liberalism.

Despite these misgivings, the prospects for the future in the world of ideas, particularly for the next few decades, are extremely bright. As I have noted, currents of opinion tend to last a long time, gaining strength for many decades before they are reversed or diverted by growing counter-currents. Our liberal ideas still share many characteristics of counter-currents rather than the main current, possibly since they have become the main current of opinion only in the past decade or so. The 'glimmerings of change' we saw in 1962 were for a time almost completely repressed and prevented from developing in the United States by the controversy over the Vietnam War. And there is every reason to expect that experience with big government will continue to add recruits to the ranks of liberalism. We have a strong foundation on which to build; numerous and able advocates; and, as noted, proliferating think-tanks.

Political stalemate

The situation is much less hopeful in the world of practical politics. The high hopes that many of us placed in the elections of Margaret Thatcher in Britain and Ronald Reagan in the United States have been realised to only a limited extent. Most of us are sorely disappointed in how limited that extent has been, how difficult it has been to translate widespread public opinion into practice, how stubborn is the 'Tyranny of the Status Quo', as my wife and I entitled our latest book.[10]

Our disappointment partly reflects naïveté. After all, it took nearly half-a-century in the United States to construct the 'New Deal', the 'Fair Deal', and then the 'Great Society'. How could we expect to dismantle it in four years? But mostly, the failure to move faster simply reflects the vested interests that have developed in government policies. General principles are one thing; narrow, private interests another. The overwhelming public vote in favour of reducing government expenditure conceals an unwillingness to accept cuts in the specific disbursements that benefit each of us. And our political structures give specific interests a considerable advantage over the general interest, as has been emphasised repeatedly.

This is not the place to discuss possible ways to counter the bias in our political structure—often summarised as 'the prisoner's dilemma'—whereby each of us acting in our own interest is led to behave in a way that ends up leaving us all worse off.[11] As we put it in *Free to Choose*:[12]

> 'In the government sphere, as in the market, there seems to be an invisible hand, but it operates in precisely the opposite direction from Adam Smith's: an individual who intends only to serve the public interest by fostering government intervention is "led by an invisible hand to promote" private interests "which was no part of his intention" '.

Nonetheless, I maintain my optimism, combined with a

[10]Harcourt Brace Jovanovich, New York and San Diego/Secker and Warburg, London, 1984.

[11]We have suggested some possibilities in both *Free to Choose* and *Tyranny of the Status Quo*.

[12]*Op. cit.*, pp. 5-6.

heightened realisation of how long it is likely to take to dismantle big government. Those of us fortunate enough to live in relatively free societies believe that the ideas of the public will ultimately determine the policies of our governments, and that special interests, while never completely conquered, will be unable completely to defeat what the public considers the general interest. As Dicey put it:[13]

> ' "Though men", to use the words of Hume, "be much governed by interest, yet even interest itself, and all human affairs, are entirely governed by *opinion*." . . . [W]here the public has influence, the development of the law must of necessity be governed by public opinion.
>
> 'But though this answer is sufficient, there exists so much misunderstanding as to the connection between men's interests and their beliefs that it is well to pursue the matter a step further. The citizens of a civilised country . . . are for the most part not recklessly selfish in the ordinary sense of that word; they wish, no doubt, to promote their own interests . . . but they certainly do not intend to sacrifice, to their own private advantage or emolument, either the happiness of their neighbours or the welfare of the State. Individuals, indeed, and still more frequently classes, do constantly support laws or institutions which they deem beneficial to themselves, but which certainly are in fact injurious to the rest of the world. But the explanation of this conduct will be found, in nine cases out of ten, to be that men come easily to believe that arrangements agreeable to themselves are beneficial to others. A man's interest gives a bias to his judgement far oftener than it corrupts his heart.'

Or, as Keynes put it in the last sentence of *The General Theory*, 'soon or late, it is ideas, not vested interests, which are dangerous for good or evil'.[14]

Optimism, then, but optimism tempered by the fear that we may be whistling in the dark. It is hard not be discouraged by the miniscule changes in policy that have so far been produced by a major change in public opinion.

---

[13]*Op. cit.*, pp. 14-15.
[14]*Op. cit.*, p. 384.

The Moral Imperative
of the Market

F. A. Hayek

F. A. Hayek

FREDERICK A. HAYEK, Dr Jur, Dr Sc Pol (Vienna), DSc (Econ.) (London), was Visiting Professor at the University of Salzburg, Austria, 1970-74. Among his previous appointments, he was Tooke Professor of Economic Science and Statistics, University of London, 1931-50; Professor of Social and Moral Science, University of Chicago, 1950-62; Professor of Economics, University of Freiburg i.Brg., West Germany, 1962-68. He was awarded the Alfred Nobel Memorial Prize in Economic Sciences in 1974. He was appointed Companion of Honour in the Queen's Birthday Honours in June 1984.

Professor Hayek's most important publications include *Prices and Production* (1931), *Monetary Theory and the Trade Cycle* (1933), *The Pure Theory of Capital* (1941), *The Road to Serfdom* (1944), *Individualism and Economic Order* (1948), *The Counter-Revolution of Science* (1952), and *The Constitution of Liberty* (1960). His latest works are collections of his writings under the titles *Studies in Philosophy, Politics and Economics* (1967), *New Studies in Philosophy, Politics, Economics and the History of Ideas* (1978), and *Law, Legislation and Liberty* (3 Vols., 1973-79).

The IEA has published his *The Confusion of Language in Political Thought* (1968), his Wincott Memorial Lecture, *Economic Freedom and Representative Government* (1973), a collection of his writings with a new essay (assembled by Sudha Shenoy), *A Tiger by the Tail* (1972, Second Edition, 1978), 'The Repercussions of Rent Restrictions' in *Verdict on Rent Control* (1972), *Full Employment at Any Price?* (1975), *Choice in Currency: A Way to Stop Inflation* (1976), *Denationalisation of Money—The Argument Refined* (1976, Second Edition, 1978), and *1980s Unemployment and the Unions* (1980).

The Moral Imperative
of the Market

F. A. HAYEK

IN 1936, the year in which (entirely coincidentally) John Maynard Keynes published *The General Theory*, I suddenly saw, as I prepared my Presidential Address to the London Economic Club, that my previous work in different branches of economics had a common root. This insight was that the price system was really an instrument which enabled millions of people to adjust their efforts to events, demands and conditions, of which they had no concrete, direct knowledge, and that the whole co-ordination of the world economy was due to certain practices and usages which had grown up unconsciously. The problem I had first identified in studying industrial fluctuations—that false price signals misdirected human efforts—I then followed up in various other branches of the discipline.

Inspiration of Ludwig von Mises

Here my thinking was inspired largely by Ludwig von Mises' conception of the problem of ordering a planned economy. My early investigation into the consequences of rent restriction showed me more clearly than almost anything else how government interference with the price system completely upsets human economic efforts.

But it took me a long time to develop what is basically a simple idea.

I was puzzled that Mises' *Socialism*,[1] which had been so convincing to me and seemed finally to show why central

[1] Yale University Press, New Haven, 1951; reprinted by New York University Press, New York, 1985.

planning could not work, had not convinced the rest of the world. I asked myself why this was the case.

Prices and economic order

I gradually found that the basic function of economics was to explain the process of how human activity adapted itself to data about which it had no information. Thus the whole economic order rested on the fact that by using prices as a guide, or as signals, we were led to serve the demands and enlist the powers and capacities of people of whom we knew nothing. It was because we had relied on a system which we had never understood and which we had never designed that we had been able to produce the wealth to sustain an enormous increase in the world's population, and to begin to realise our new ambitions of distributing this wealth more justly. Basically, the insight that prices were signals bringing about the unforeseen co-ordination of the efforts of thousands of individuals was in a sense the modern cybernetics theory, and it became the leading idea behind my work.

It forced me inevitably to investigate the relationship between current political beliefs and the preservation of the system on which the wealth of which we are so inordinately proud depends. Although Adam Smith, like Marshall 150 years later, had basically grasped the point that the success of our economic system was the outcome of an undesigned process co-ordinating the activities of a myriad of individuals, he never fully convinced the leaders of public opinion of this truth. This has become my chief task, and it has taken me something like 50 years to be able to put it as briefly and in as few words as I have just attempted; even 10 years ago I could not have put it as succinctly. It seems obvious, once it is stated, that the basic foundation of our civilisation and our wealth is a system of signals which informs us, however imperfectly, of the effects of millions of events which occur in the world, to which we have to adapt ourselves and about which we may have no direct information.

Improving the market system

This insight has extraordinarily important consequences once its truth has been accepted. Either you must confine yourself to creating an institutional framework within which the price system will operate as efficiently as possible, or you are driven to upsetting its function. If it is true that prices are signals which enable us to adapt our activities to *unknown* events and demands, it is evidently nonsense to believe that we can control prices. You cannot improve a signal if you do not know what it signals. It is not inconsistent to admit that the price system, even in the theory of a perfectly competitive market, does not take account of all the things that we would like to be taken into account. But if we cannot improve upon the system by directly interfering with prices, we can try to find new methods of feeding information into the market which has not previously been taken into account.

There is still ample room for progress in this direction. Furthermore, beyond what the market already does for us, there is ample opportunity for using deliberate organisation to 'fill in' what the market cannot provide. Thus we get the best out of the market only if we try to improve the framework within which it operates. We have to go outside the market system to make provision (through government and other organisations) for those people who are not in a position to look after themselves.

Socialism: an intellectual error

This line of argument raises some very serious intellectual and moral problems. In the first instance, it seems to me that the ambitions of socialism reflect intellectual error rather than different values. Socialism is based on the lack of understanding of what it is to which we owe the available wealth that socialists hope to redistribute. This objection raises certain other issues which I began to sketch out in a lecture I gave in 1978[2] at the London School of Economics. The central

[2] 'The Three Sources of Human Values', published as an Epilogue to *Law, Legislation and Liberty*, Vol. 3: *The Political Order of a Free People*, Routledge and Kegan Paul, London, 1979, pp. 153-176.

problem was the conflict between our inborn emotions about laws acquired in a primitive small society, where small groups of people served known fellows for common purposes, and the changes in morals which had to take place to make possible the worldwide division of labour.

Indeed, this small development, which took mankind over 3,000 years gradually to effect, involved very largely a deliberate suppression of very strong emotional feelings which we all have in our bones and of which we cannot entirely rid ourselves. I shall illustrate this briefly with reference to the idea which still prevails about solidarity. Agreement about a common purpose between a group of known people is clearly an idea that cannot be applied to a large society which includes people who do not know one another. The modern society and the modern economy have grown up through the recognition that this idea, which was fundamental to life in a small group—a face-to-face society, is simply inapplicable to large groups. The essential basis of the development of modern civilisation is to allow people to pursue their own ends on the basis of their own knowledge and not be bound by the aims of other people.

Mirage of social justice

The same dilemma applies to the basic desire of socialism for distribution according to principles of justice. If prices are to serve as an effective guide to what people ought to do, you cannot reward people for what are or were their good intentions. You must allow prices to be determined so as to tell people where they can make the best contribution to the rest of society—and unfortunately the capacity of making good contributions to one's fellows is not distributed according to any principles of justice. People are in a very unequal position to make contributions to the requirements of their fellows and have to choose between very different opportunities. In order therefore to enable them to adapt themselves to a structure which they do not know (and the determinants of which they do not know), we have to allow the spontaneous mechanisms of the market to tell them what they ought to do.

It was a sad mistake in the history of economics which prevented economists, particularly the classical economists, from seeing that the essential function of prices was to tell people what they ought to do in the future and that prices could not be based on what they had done in the past. Our modern insight is that prices are signals which inform people of what they ought to do in order to adjust themselves to the rest of the system.

I am now profoundly convinced of what I had only hinted at before, namely, that the struggle between the advocates of a free society and the advocates of the socialist system is not a moral but an *intellectual* conflict. Thus socialists have been led by a very peculiar development to revive certain primitive instincts and feelings which in the course of hundreds of years had been practically suppressed by commercial or mercantile morals, which by the middle of the last century had come to govern the world economy.

The decline of commercial morality

Until 130 or 150 years ago, everybody in what is now the industrialised part of the Western world grew up acquainted with the rules and necessities of what are called commercial or mercantile morals, because everyone worked in a small enterprise where he was equally concerned with, and exposed to, the conduct of others. Whether as master or servant or member of the family, everybody accepted the unavoidable necessity of having to adapt himself to changes in demand, supply and prices in the market-place. A change began to happen in the middle of the last century. Where previously perhaps only the aristocracy and its servants were strangers to the rules of the market, the growth of large organisations in business, commerce, finance, and ultimately in government, increased the number of people who grew up without being taught the morals of the market which had been developed in the course of the preceding 2,000 years.

For probably the first time since classical antiquity, an ever-increasing part of the population of the modern industrial state grew up without learning in childhood that it was indispensable to respond as both producer and consumer to all the unpleasant things which the changing market required. This development coincided with the spreading of a new philosophy, which taught people that they ought not to submit to any principle of morals which could not be rationally justified. I think it was true that, with the exception of a few men like Adam Smith (and with him to only a limited extent), nobody before the middle of the 19th century could really have answered the question: Why should we obey these moral principles which have never been rationally justified? The failure of a large number of people to accept the moral principles which form the basis of the capitalist system was supported by a new intellectual trend which taught them that these morals had no rational justification.

Ideals versus survival

This dichotomy explains the increasing opposition to the market system that has expanded far beyond the specifically socialist parties of the last century. In the course of history almost every step in the development of commercial morals had to be contested against the opposition of moral philosophers and religious teachers—a story well enough known in its outlines. We are now in the extraordinary situation that, while we live in a world with a large and growing population which can be kept alive thanks only to the prevalence of the market system, the vast majority of people (I do not exaggerate) no longer believes in the market. It is a crucial question for the future preservation of civilisation and one which must be faced before the arguments of socialism return us to a primitive morality. We must again suppress those innate feelings which have welled up in us once we ceased to learn the taut discipline of the market, before they destroy our capacity to feed the population through the co-ordinating system of the market. Otherwise, the collapse of capitalism will ensure that a very large part of the world's population will die because we cannot feed it.

This is a serious problem, and one which has not had to be solved in the past. The world's population, and not even the leading minds in any one country, will never be persuaded by theoretical argument that they ought to believe in a certain kind of morality. We can nonetheless demonstrate that unless people are willing to submit to the discipline constituted by commercial morals, our capacity to support any further growth of population other than in the relatively prosperous West, or even to maintain it at its existing numbers, will be destroyed.

I would not agree that the process of selection by which the morals of capitalism have evolved, producing what a few text-books acknowledge as its 'beneficial effects on society at large', consists wholly in assisting the growth of population. Many of the world's peoples would probably be much happier if population growth had not been stimulated to the degree that it has. Nonetheless, the world's population has grown to a size where it can be fed only by adhering to a market system. Attempts to replace the market demonstrate—most graphically in Ethiopia—the folly of imposing an alternative.

As prosperity has led the more advanced peoples voluntarily to restrict the growth of population, so those peoples who are only very slowly beginning to learn this urgent lesson may come to see that it is not in their interests to grow more rapidly. At this critical juncture for the kind of civilisation that we have built up, the most important contribution an economist can make is to insist that we can fulfil our responsibility to sustain our existing population only by continuing to rely on the market system, which brought this enlarged population into existence in the first place.

Principal Writings of Arthur Seldon

Everyman's Dictionary of Economics (with F. G. Pennance), J. M. Dent, London, 1965; 2nd Edition 1975.

The Great Pensions 'Swindle', Tom Stacey Books, London, 1970.

Charge, Maurice Temple Smith, London, 1977.

Socialism Explained, Sherwood Press, London, 1983 (US edition: *Socialism: The Grand Delusion*, Universe Books, New York, 1986).

Capitalism, Blackwell, Oxford (forthcoming).

Primer on Public Choice (with C. K. Rowley), Blackwell, Oxford (forthcoming).

The Liberal Impulse, Maurice Temple Smith/Gower, Aldershot, Hants. (forthcoming).

EDITOR:

The Litmus Papers: A National Health Dis-service, Centre for Policy Studies, London, 1980.

The 'New Right' Enlightenment, E & L Books, Sevenoaks, Kent, 1985.

CONTRIBUTIONS:

'Which Way to Welfare?', *Lloyds Bank Review*, October 1966.

'The Lessons of Centralised Medicine', in *New Directions in Public Health Care*, Institute for Contemporary Studies, San Francisco, 1976.

'Individual Liberty, Public Goods and Representative Democracy', in *Ordo*, Vol. 30, Gustav Fischer Verlag, Stuttgart, 1979.

'The Next Thirty Years . . .?', in *National Health Issues: The British Experience*, Roche Laboratories, 1980.

Writings for the Institute of Economic Affairs

Pensions in a Free Society, 1957.

Pensions for Prosperity, Hobart Paper 4, 1960.

Taxation and Welfare, Research Monograph 14, 1967.

After the NHS, Occasional Paper 21, 1968.

Corrigible Capitalism, Incorrigible Socialism, Occasional Paper 57, 1980.

Wither the Welfare State, Occasional Paper 60, 1981.

The Riddle of the Voucher, Hobart Paperback 21, 1986.

*   *   *

with R. Harris and M. Naylor, *Hire Purchase in a Free Society*, 1958; 3rd Edition 1961.

with Ralph Harris:

Advertising in a Free Society, 1959.

Advertising in Action, 1962.

Advertising and the Public, 1962.

Choice in Welfare 1970, 1971.

Pricing or Taxing?, Hobart Paper 71, 1976.

Not from Benevolence . . ., Hobart Paperback 10, 1977.

Over-Ruled on Welfare, Hobart Paperback 13, 1979.

Shoppers' Choice?, Occasional Paper 68, 1984.

with Hamish Gray, *Universal or Selective Social Benefits?*, Research Monograph 8, 1967.

*   *   *

CONTRIBUTED TO:

Policy for Poverty, Research Monograph 20, 1970.

Catch '76 . . .?, Occasional Paper 47, 1976.

The Coming Confrontation, Hobart Paperback 12, 1978.

The Taming of Government, IEA Readings 21, 1979.

*   *   *

Editor of *Economic Affairs* since its inception in 1980.